MW01095086

The Average Surfer's Guide

To Travel, Waves, and Progression

Simon Short

ISBN: 1985861887
ISBN-13: 978-1985861886

Cover Photograph Copyright © 2019 by Stephanie Hernandez
Cover design by S.Short with KDP
Editing by Diana Bravo at Bravo Edit
Author photograph by @average_surfers_guide
Interior photograph at Trestles by Garrett Fermo

The information in this book is meant to supplement, not replace, proper surf and ocean training. Like any sport involving speed, equipment, balance, and environmental factors, surfing poses some inherent risk. The authors and publisher advise readers to take full responsibility for their safety and know their limits. Before practicing the skills described in this book, be sure that your equipment is well maintained, and do not take risks beyond your level of experience, aptitude, training, and comfort level. Although the author and publisher have made every effort to ensure that the information in this book was correct at press time, the author and publisher do not assume and hereby disclaim any liability to any party for any loss, damage, or disruption caused by errors or omissions, whether such errors or omissions result from negligence, accident, or any other cause. This book is not intended as a substitute for the medical advice of physicians. The reader should regularly consult a physician in matters relating to his/her health and particularly with respect to any symptoms that may require diagnosis or medical attention.

DEDICATION

This is for every surfer who, in their own mind, has equal moments of brilliance and frustration.

CHAPTERS

ACKNOWLEDGMENTS

A million thanks to many wonderful people. To my surfing brothers and sisters, Phil, Boris, Nick, Mark, Derek, Jason, Sam, Garrett, Uyen, Chris, Steph, and Mike.
Stephanie, for your photo and for being you.
To Simon and Dave at Fitzroy Surfboards for making amazing boards and environmentally conscious clothing.
Diana Bravo at Bravo edit. Zach and Juan at The Inertia for publishing my writing and Spy Optics for supporting The Adventures of an Average Surfer.

*"AUTUMN WATERS OF THIS WORLD,
AWAKEN ME FROM MY DRUNKENNESS."*

-UNKNOWN POET

*"YOU AIN'T GONNA GET BARRELED WITH THAT
ATTITUDE, MATE."*

-STRANGER WHO CALLED ME OUT FOR NOT GOING
ON A SET WAVE

Author's Note

This book was born from an article I wrote titled "A Story About Surfing, Depression and Identity," published in 2016 on theinertia.com. I wrote the article simply to be productive and creative after a difficult time in my life and to get my thoughts on paper, where they often make more sense.

A few months after publication, the article had been shared over 5,000 times and appeared on mental health websites and blogs. I was humbled and elated that my simple writings had a positive impact on readers. The article appears in part in this book, as do other articles I've written that have been published online.

This book became a collection of follow up thoughts from the original article and tackles many issues, both positive and negative, relating to surfing and life.

All stories and lessons in this book are true accounts from memory. The perceived advice given is from research and experience and no formal education in psychology.

We are all on a journey and can learn lessons from one another both in and out of water.

AN AVERAGE SURFER

I was fifteen when I first started surfing in South West England. Back then, it didn't matter what the conditions were, my friends and I would venture out into anything. I remember sessions when ice and frost had formed on the ground in the parking lot, and the onshore gale force winds were howling under dark gray skies. It didn't matter to us, we were always stoked for the adventure.

These days, I'm an average surfer. I've surfed for over eighteen years and spent most of those years at the same skill level. There seems to be a similar pattern at play in most surfers' progression patterns, and there comes a point where we plateau at an intermediate level. We then become "the average surfer." I have good days and bad days in the ocean. I try to surf as much as possible, but sometimes I make excuses to avoid going out into the waves. I may convince myself that the waves are too small or too big, the ocean is too cold, or the winds are onshore. I must admit, I have become a bit spoiled when it comes to surfing. I prefer to surf under sunny, blue skies, and I thrive in three-to-four-foot surf. I start to wobble and get butterflies once the waves start to top head-high.

I moved to Southern California ten years ago and now live in Huntington Beach, a fun little surf town situated about twenty miles from Disneyland. The best thing for me about Huntington Beach is that you can bank on something surfable at least three hundred days out of the year. Maybe more. While the quality of waves offered is not world class, the consistency is. It's a far cry from the fickle conditions of my youth in the West Country of England.

Huntington Beach started as an oil town. One can look at old black and white photographs from the twentieth century and see a landscape of nothing but oil rigs, nodding donkeys, and oil worker accommodations. Most of those accommodations are still visible today, situated along the numbered streets disguised as overpriced duplexes. The town boomed in the 1960s, and as the oil dried up, tourism flooded in.

Today, downtown Huntington Beach is an interesting mix of wealthy, conservative, second-home owners, upper middle-class families, and beach bums. To a certain extent, it can still hold its reputation from the 1980s and 90s as a seedy, slimy town where biker gangs roam, drunkenness is rampant, and odd riots takes place. But, really, Huntington Beach is a tourist-filled surf town trying desperately to modernize and become the vacation destination of wealthy yacht owners. For every luxury hotel that is built along the Pacific Coast Highway is another young surfer willing to pay extortionate rent to move into a studio apartment in the downtown streets. Like many Southern California beach towns, Huntington Beach will always find itself between beach bum and luxury living.

Most surfers seem to spend the first two years or so learning the basics. We practice the pop-up over and over while torpedoing towards the beach with a reckless abandon for any poor soul that dare lay before us. Then one day it happens. The moment. The moment that hooks most of us for life. Somehow you end up on the clean, green face of the wave, riding parallel to the beach. It's a completely new experience. A wonderfully different feeling to the turbulence of the whitewater and the straight lines we were drawing for those last months and years. If you are lucky, that new experience will last a few seconds, maybe more. However long it lasts, that moment of transition, of brilliance, that moment of wisdom and inspiration, has the power to change lives.

I was sixteen when I encountered that moment that would change my life forever. I had been surfing for a year at the time. My friends and I would surf as much as we could back then, and we taught ourselves because surf schools just weren't cool, or so we thought in our youthful arrogance. My good friend, Boris Morris, and I were at Saunton Sands Beach in North Devon. Boris was one from a group of best friends I surfed with in my teenage years. He was burly, even at seventeen years old, and stood about six feet tall but still had the appearance of being stocky. His brown hair changed styles with the seasons, from dreadlocks, to cropped, to unkempt hippy. He had tattoos on his arms and wore Stussy t-shirts, baggy jeans, and a metal bead necklace. If that sounds awful, that's because it was, but as this was the early 2000s, his style fit perfectly.

It was a typical gray spring day in Saunton. The daytime air was warm enough for a light sweatshirt and promised the approach of summer. Saunton is a three-and-a-half-mile stretch of sand bordered by the ocean on one side and endless sand dunes on the other. It's a great wave for beginners and a fantastic longboarding wave because of its long, sloping walls and mellow crowds. The waves on this day were knee high, and the wind strength was light with cross shore conditions. The waves were still breaking cleanly, and, as always, Boris and I were excited to paddle out.

We had been surfing for about forty minutes when I paddled into the already broken wave that would change my life. With the whitewater tumbling towards the beach, I was frantically paddling to catch it. The wave caught up to me and gave me the first bump from behind, and I felt the familiar acceleration of my borrowed eight-foot Superfrog surfboard, adorned with yellowing foam, dents, and holes. (The board belonged to Boris, but he was using a newer one he'd recently purchased.) I pushed down on the board with my arms, and with the grace of a newborn goat finding its legs, I scrambled to my feet. It wasn't pretty. First, one leg began to protrude outwards, then the other from behind, until I gently eased myself up on the board and into a standing position as the whitewater wave raced me towards land. The frantic paddle to scrambled pop-up was a routine performance by me at this point. Once on my feet I assumed a position I liked to call the "big kahuna stance." This stance was similar to the stance taken by dark-skinned Hawaiian legends like Eddie Aikau, who in videos appeared graceful amongst the chaos of racing down forty and fifty-foot wave faces in the Pacific Islands. You know the stance—legs wide apart, low center of gravity, and arms out like a gull. Only *my* wave was a two-foot mush burger, not fierce and deadly like Waimea Bay.

As I raced towards the beach like I had done numerous times before, something changed in the air. The wave began to get bigger and reform. Instead of dying out like it usually did, the wave was growing, and I was being lifted. *Holy crap*, I thought, *what's happening?* I lowered my butt towards the sun-beaten Superfog, widened my feet, and kept my arms out. The next thing I knew I was going in a diagonal direction, and my board was dropping down a slide of smooth, green water. It felt like the fastest, baddest, most awesome thing anyone had ever done on a surfboard. Thankfully, this was pre-invention of the GoPro, so my delusions remained intact for some years.

After I dropped down the wave, there I was, out on the face. No more whitewater. No more turbulence. No more straight lines. This was different; this was smooth and green. The ride felt like nothing I had ever experienced, like walking on water. I kept going, the wave propelling me towards the beach, and for the first time in my short surfing life I felt like I had some control. I leaned down further and put my hand in the wall of the wave like I had seen my favorite surfer, Dave Rastovich, do in a movie. That was when I fell face first. The moment was done. I didn't know at the time, but my life had just changed forever. I stood up in knee-high water and hoped Boris had witnessed the best wave of my life. But, of course, he hadn't.

Not everyone reacts the same way to moments of greatness. I've seen it time and time again in my later experiences as a surfing instructor. I have also seen human beings who somehow seem to be immune from surfing. Those people are a minority in that they remain as regular humans even after they are exposed to the green face. They somehow go back to their respective everyday lives and manage to file their surfing experiences away in the back of their brain, alongside that time they went rock climbing in high school or kayaking in the harbor. For that immune class of humans, the moment was just another fun activity for them. They might return to the ocean once or twice a year, but they don't become surfers. I almost envy this class of special beings. They're able to go on with their lives without the constant calling from the ocean lingering in the back of their minds.

The remainder of us, well, we are left chasing the dragon for the rest of our lives. Every decision we make from that moment on will subconsciously be made with the waves in mind. You might apply for a job but decide not to take it because the long commute would leave you short on surfing time.

You'll wonder if that house or apartment you were looking at is close enough to the waves. Maybe if you woke up at 5 a.m. you could get a quick session in and still be at the office on time. That car you just bought will surely have enough space for your boards. All those decisions were made because of surfing. We are all hooked, my friends.

There are many of us who suffer. Some you can easily recognize on the street with their sun kissed hair, tanned skin, and red, salty eyes. Others are stealthier, and you wouldn't know they were part of our tribe unless you saw them in the lineup. From doctors to trash collectors, male and female, young and old, it doesn't matter, we are all "slaves to the waves." Once we come to terms with that fact, we can accept the absolute blessing and gift we have been given as surfers. But, as life moves us forward, it can become more and more difficult to fit surfing into our adult lives. It can also become more difficult to define, reason, or even defend why surfing has such a hold on us as grown men and women. It is easy to explain why surfing plays such an important role in your life if you are involved in the industry or a professional, but what if you are the average surfer working nine-to-five? How do we get to surf every day and travel to far off lands like the professionals?

Surfing can be so many different things to so many people. It can be an art form, a stress reliever, a profession, a technical sport, a community, or a lifestyle. Learning where to put your board on a wave, where the power and speed is, and how to best interlace the turns and maneuver with grace is what keeps us coming back for more. Time after time we return to the waves. Winter, summer, rain or shine, we always go back.

It only takes one wave to make a great session. That one wave where the wave opens and lets you in. You ride from top to bottom and back to the pocket. You make it to the inside and calmly cruise over the back of the wave to end the ride. We've all had those magic waves where everything just went right without much thinking, the waves that give you the energy to paddle back out with your head held high and a beaming smile. These waves become stories told for years.

On the contrary, we also experience the bad days where we are frustrated or annoyed with ourselves or the conditions. The days where it just won't work, and you can't get any good waves. You've paddled for what seems like the perfect shoulder, and it just won't let you in. Right at the last minute you can see the wall lining up, and you fall off the back of the wave and splash the water in sheer irritation. What's to blame this time? Wrong board? The conditions? Yourself?

On my best days, I can string some decent turns together and a cutback or two. On my worst days, I don't catch a single good wave and cuss to myself. A lot. Like I said, I'm the average surfer, but I love and need surfing, just like so many others do.

So, where does the "average surfer" land in the lineup? Take a closer look at your local surf spot, you can usually place the surfers there in one of three groups. First, there are the beginners, easily identifiable by their bright, soft boards, flapping arms, legs spread apart, and general sense of glee, fear, and wonderment at the waves and ocean around them. Next are the experts or professionals. They come in all shapes and sizes but are easily identifiable by their grace and ease in the water. This group makes everything look easy. Some are young with sponsors and logos on their boards, others may be old with years of dedication and local knowledge behind them. Either way, the expert group usually makes up a small percentage of the lineup. They spend a lot of time in the water, although they usually keep to themselves.

In between these two groups you will find the lineup's majority—the rest of us, the average surfers. The title "average surfer" shouldn't be taken in a negative connotation. Average simply means a number expressing the central value in a set of data. In this case, the value is the skill set of surfers. We have moments of brilliance and can hold our own in many surfing arenas, we can also appear frustrated and nervous when we let our insecurities get the best of us. The most notable thing about the "average" group is its size. It's huge. Without a doubt, we are the majority. We are the core of surf culture in every aspect. We support the surf industry and buy the most boards, wetsuits, and wax. We read all the surf magazines and watch all the surf movies. Forget the glamor and pomp of professional surfing, the average surfer *is* surfing.

So, if we are the largest demographic in the surf community, why are we so ignored? Surfing is sold and marketed predominantly to the former two groups—beginner and expert. If you are just beginning on your surfing journey there are numerous books, videos, and camps available and aimed towards beginners. On the other hand, when I see movies, pictures, and especially travel articles about a beautiful, far-off destination like Indonesia, Hawaii, or South Africa, everything seems to be aimed at an advanced surfer who is capable of handling huge waves and fast barrels better than myself or most average surfers I see in my local lineup. I understand that surf and travel companies want to market themselves the best way they can. A magazine won't bother publishing a picture of an average four-foot day that looks suitable for my average skill set when they can publish the day of all days—double overhead waves with a professional surfer riding a potato chip spacecraft board and tucked up in a huge barrel. I get it, but why not have more balance and truth in coverage and marketing? Why not appeal to most surfers of an intermediate skill set?

One of the issues with being an average surfer is the size of the group. As an average surfer, your skill set can span so many levels. You can identify as average if you surfed for a year and are still learning to trim on a wave. You can also identify as average if you have surfed for ten years and can link a few sections together.

As an average surfer, one side of my brain is excited

at the prospect and challenge of surfing at far off destinations while the other side lets my insecurities tell me I'm not good enough to surf some of those places, sometimes even at my local breaks on bigger days. Some years ago, I decided to ignore my insecurities and start a new surfing journey. I was sick of telling myself I used to be a better surfer when I was younger. There was no reason why I couldn't be a better surfer in my thirties than I was in my twenties. I started a whole new approach to surfing and life. I took it back to basics and began cultivating an appetite to learn and progress again. It was a matter of no longer being complacent or accepting my intermediate surfing standard. I had to face many challenges and become more self-aware than ever before, both in life and in the water.

Over the next few years, I explored some great surf destinations around the world, learned new techniques and philosophies, and studied the affect that fear had on my surfing, all while learning new ways to progress. Some of those lessons were learned through more contemporary outlets such a books, podcasts, and videos. Other lessons were learned unwittingly or by circumstances I had no control of in my personal life.

In 2015, after some extremely difficult years and dark times that led to severe depression, I went on a journey to learn more about myself and how to balance my life. Other questions came up along the way, like why surfing had had such an extensive, far reaching role in my life. The journey began with the aim of doing things that made me happiest in life and becoming a more positive and giving person. I began to learn that surfing was an amazing counterweight to balance the scales of life. With that in mind, I wanted to be able to paddle out anywhere in the world and get better waves. I no longer wanted to be just an average surfer. I hoped not only to become a better surfer but also a better person.

IDENTITY AND VALUE SYSTEMS

Like most modern-day surfers, I started surfing because it just looked so appealing. I remember growing up in Southwest England and seeing tanned surfers driving around town in their sticker-covered vans. They always seemed to have a laid back vibe about them. I also remember watching the local weather forecasts and hearing the weatherman speak some strange language about tides, buoys, and wave heights that was covertly directed at a few surfers and fishermen who understood. The whole lifestyle and community were inviting. The secret language, the adventure, the travel, the boards, the waves, and the clothes were all so foreign yet so tempting.

As I dipped my toe into the lifestyle at the age of fifteen, I wanted more and more. I not only longed for the ride and the exuberance but also the feeling of belonging to a tribe. Later in my surfing life I learned that surfing is quite an isolated activity, but at fifteen, most are looking for some sense of identity and belonging. Surfing became mine. I joined the tribe and am still a fully-fledged, card carrying member today.

In my early surfing days, I had about ten friends I surfed with regularly. We spent every weekend for about four years or so loading surfboards into our vans and heading down the motorway for two hours towards Devon or Cornwall to surf our brains out. We would leave after work on a Friday night and come back late Sunday. On Saturdays we would often surf for six hours in the morning and three hours in the afternoon. We slept in our vans and woke up to do it all over again the next day. Surfing was all we cared about, and most of us put off college and worked in factory or construction jobs from Monday to Friday just to earn enough money to camp and surf on weekends. We were the quintessential weekend warriors.

As the years went on our surfing crew became inevitably smaller. One by one my friends stopped surfing; some may have been the immune humans I mentioned earlier. Others let life and responsibilities take over. They found themselves surfing less due to work, college, commitments, or lack of motivation. I am positive they still long for the waves and have that same feeling I get every time they see the ocean.

Now, almost eighteen years later, there are four of us left from that same group who remain as die-hard surfers. All four of us are full blown addicts. We live in different parts of the world, but every phone conversation or email usually starts with the same question, "You get any good waves lately?" It will always unite us. On the rare occasions we meet up somewhere it will be for a surf trip as we continue to make incredible memories around this amazing sport and lifestyle. Surfing, while mainly solitary, can be a primal bonding experience between friends, especially on days where the waves are bigger. There is nothing like experiencing big waves with friends. Whatever "big" means to you is irrelevant. What matters is watching each other's defeats and successes and feeling each other's pain and joy. There is a pure and simple feeling of survival amongst friends when you walk out of the ocean together and back to your vehicles after paddling through Mother Nature's wrath. It is a true Victory at Sea moment.

Since those early years my life has subconsciously been shaped around surfing. All the major changes in my life were indirectly linked to the activity. I've spent the last ten years of my life living six thousand miles away from home in South West England so that I could surf more frequently. My mood is influenced by surfing, and my business is now shaped by it too.

I am currently thirty-three years old and have lived in Orange County, California for ten years. Orange County couldn't be any more of a contrast to where I grew up. South West England is sparse, rural, and fairly remote. It's open, rugged, and beautiful with green fields and shady, dark skies. It is harsh yet cozy. You can easily find space to yourself. The surfing scene, while popular in summer, is still somewhat underground and close-knit. You can hike a cliff line and not see another soul for miles, especially in winter. I love England, it will always be home.

Somewhat conflicting is the fact that I also love Southern California, which includes the densely populated and crawling with consumerism and selfishness Orange County. One can easily assume that Southern California is all traffic, strip malls, and concrete. However, once you scratch beneath the surface, you will find incredible open spaces, woodlands, rivers, and beaches. You can live a life of plenty and have as much or as little as you desire. It is a place where you need to keep yourself in check and remember not to neglect your spiritual side. If you don't get swallowed by the fast pace of life and glorification of status, then it is one of the best places to live in the world, and the excellent weather is always a plus.

I spent my first few years in California distracted with doing what I thought I was supposed to do; I had a career, a three-bedroom house, a wife, and a car payment. At the age of twenty-seven, I had everything but kids. I sacrificed surfing and lived two hours from the nearest ocean. I surfed once or twice a year, at best. I was doing the responsible thing, and, to be honest, I had never been more miserable in my entire life. The pressure of society's demands weighed hard on my shoulders. I believed that status equaled success, which in turn equaled happiness. I was a law enforcement officer, which became my identity, and surfing was a fringe activity that stole valuable time from real life. But why was I unhappy? Not only was I unhappy, I was extremely depressed and pretending to be fine.

As I continued down my chosen path a shadow began to follow me. I wasn't myself, my mood was dark, and my thoughts became negative. My relationship was essentially dead, and my behavior and mood became increasingly erratic. As the years passed, I fell deeper into the hole. I began to feel more and more uncomfortable. There was a deep, inner voice that told me I wasn't being true to myself and hinted at the need for me to make changes. I kept ignoring it and continued to use negative coping skills to distract myself. As the voice loudened the depression darkened, but I continued with my life pretending to be ok. No matter how much I would pretend to be fine, I knew that I would eventually have to make a decision—and none of the options were easy.

It was fall of 2013 when I had one of my darkest moments. It was also the catalyst for me to begin to change. On Halloween night my partner and I were on patrol in a desert town near Palm Springs, California. I wanted to be a police officer since the age of five. My grandad had a huge influence on me. He was a copper on the River Thames for the London Metropolitan Police Force in the 1960s. It was a family tradition that dated back over three generations before him. I always imagined my grandad being an upstanding, community-orientated officer and the kind of man that treated everyone fairly. That was the kind of police officer I wanted to be. I soon faced the reality of modern American policing and learned that it is very different.

On that Halloween night my partner spotted a young male that he knew had an outstanding warrant for his arrest. We flipped a U-turn in our black and white patrol vehicle as the male tried to get away. He was on a BMX bike, and we were in pursuit at low speeds. I will never forget the sound I heard while on that pursuit—a strange, loud wail as the kid, who was no more than eighteen years old, cried his eyes out as he rode through the neighborhood streets. We caught up to the young man and apprehended him. He sat on the ground and continued to ball his eyes out. It was clear that he had special needs. I was mocked by two other officers for helping the kid by taking his ear buds out and trying to calm him. I always tried to be nice to everyone while working that job; I gave everyone respect as a human, even if they were going to jail. The problem is that modern policing doesn't cure anything, it's merely a Band-Aid for society's true issues. While I feel that I helped many people and made a difference as a police officer, the main focus was to go after drugs, gang members, and guns. We were just part of a cycle that helped keep young men and women in a judicial system they couldn't escape. The poor kid with special needs was an extreme example of that. I quickly learned that the world can be a violent place, and sometimes you can't be kind.

I never wanted the uniform to change me, but it is difficult to stay positive when you see the worst situations offered by society on a daily basis. Modern policing is one of the hardest jobs on Earth. There are many great men and women who are police officers, but it would take an extremely strong individual to remain unaffected by the job. The last thing I needed at the time was to forge an identity based on that occupation.

After the Halloween incident I knew I no longer wanted to do the job. It culminated a month later when my partner and I were ambushed and shot at. We responded to a call of an abandoned stolen vehicle in the desert. The location of the vehicle was adjacent to an extremely dangerous and gang riddled neighborhood. It was neighborhood that we wouldn't enter unless we had an extra patrol unit to respond with us.

As my partner and I got out of our patrol car to inspect the stolen vehicle, we heard gunshots begin to ring out in the night air and rounds were landing around us. I remember taking cover behind the vehicle and feeling strangely calm. I realized then that I didn't care if I died that night. There was nothing left inside me. That was a problem and two months later I had resigned and the people who had shot at us from the neighborhood were never located.

I learned a hard lesson in the truth of not being able to hide from yourself or the longing for what gives you a sense of belonging. It took almost five years, but I got the message loud and clear as I slowly slipped into that severe, dark hole in my mind. Having an unbalanced life resulted in the loss of my home, possessions, and career, a divorce, an awful depression, tension with my family in England, and another terrible relationship. I realized that all my choices in life led me to these things.

After leaving my career, I made another decision that was the hardest thing I have ever done. I decided to walk away from everything. My relationship was over and I was alone. I was at my lowest point, living in a shady budget motel in Anaheim with all my worldly possessions stuffed into the trunk of a rented Ford Focus. My divorce had taken everything, and I had no one left. I was six thousand miles from home, suicidal, and too proud to ask for help or go home. What was to blame? The short answer is, *I* was, and surfing helped me realize that.

Those troublesome and painful times in my life took me on an inevitable journey of self-exploration. I tried to identify who I was and what made me happy while also trying to understand the negativity, pain, and anger that lived inside me. I did everything anyone recommended. I went surfing. I read Buddhist teachings and books of meaning like *Siddhartha* and *The Old Man and the Sea*. I dove into self-help books and attachment science. I went to therapy. I took antidepressant medications. I had every opinion and theory about life thrown at me. It all helped, and I learned an awful lot. What I learned about myself is that simple is fine. I don't need the big house, the car, or the career. I needed four things to start rebuilding my life and myself: honesty, self-awareness, balance, and the ocean. I needed to stop neglecting my true self.

I remember one piece of text written by Jeff Foster that left a deep impression on me and helped me overcome depression. I often think of this text as the one thing that cured me from that horrible mental jail cell. In truth, all the readings, learnings, and medications probably helped, but this passage changed my way of thinking instead of trying to "fix" myself and get back to "normal." What if, instead of seeking normality, I had to change and be completely honest with myself?

"Perhaps our depression is not a sickness but a call to break out, to let go, to lose the old structures and stories we have been holding up about ourselves and the world and rest deeply in the truth of who we really are...What if you need to shed your half-shed skin, not climb back into it? What if sadness, and pain, and fear, and all of the waves in life's ocean, just want to move in you, to finally express themselves creatively and not be pushed   away?"
-Jeff Foster

For me, this meant no longer pretending. Even when one thinks we are living a truth, we can be suppressing a true longing for life and what really makes us get up and enjoy each day. It is very easy to suppress truths and feel fine. I think many people do this their whole lives. I learned that it was ok to ditch that particular career and the big house. It was time to identify what I *really* and *truly* needed to make me happy in life. In some respects, I felt like I had wasted five years. Really, it just took five years to learn a valuable lesson about balance.

We often hear that successful people aren't immune to depression and suicide. We are shocked when someone who seems to have it all ends their life by their own hand. This does not just apply to celebrities, it could be anyone. I suffered my darkest depression when I was deemed to be at my most successful by our western culture's grading curve of success. Status is the highest held value in the U.S. and most of western Europe. I believe this is a health hazard and likely the root cause of depression and suicide.

Materialism, consumption, and false individualism build the foundation of a dangerous value system held in the highest regard amongst most western societies. The reason we should not be shocked when a "successful" person suffers from depression is because what we often gauge as success does not equal true, fulfilling happiness. As humans we require a balance of needs, and, unfortunately, our scales tend to be weighed down on one end by materialism and consumerism while spirituality, community, and belonging are left on the sidelines. We become materialistic in the pursuit of individualism. In the beginning, the intent of individualism was a good one. We wanted to be individuals and our true selves. Unfortunately, we have been steered off course by the systems of consumption we have in place. I believe this started just after the counterculture movements of the 1960s when we had a generation of people who were anti-conformists and wanted to be free to be themselves. As the movement spread and popularized to a more subdued mainstream, industries saw opportunity to sell more products, giving us more choices to be individuals. Somehow, that led us to attach importance to possessions and money, and these things were interpreted as key factors to success and happiness. Materialism and a value system that promotes these things underpins our consumption-based economy. In reality, materialism is not associated with happiness but rather with anxiety, depression, anger, isolation, and, in the worst cases, suicide.

After my worst bout of depression, I started to notice the scale. On one side you have the value system of status, money, and one's career. On the other side you have the value system of spirituality, belonging, pleasure, and identity. We can't be balanced if we lean too far either way. As much as I would like to lean all the way and live for pleasure by living in a van and surfing every day, I don't think it would fulfill me in the long-term. It would likely be just the same if I leaned all the way towards the other side and only lived for my status, money, and career. I would always long for the other. Creating balance is key. You must enjoy life while being responsible. It takes an ongoing journey of honesty and self-awareness to keep this balance.

I am sure we all know many individuals who love their career and the status and material possessions it can bring. I am sure they work extremely hard. I would also wager that if they were completely stripped away, self-aware, and honest with themselves they would be lacking a lot from the other side of the scale. It would take a rare and special kind of person to climb the status ladder without sacrificing certain spiritual and metaphysical needs. These are the needs that are often neglected in modern Western life. There is plenty of research leading to the conclusion that this neglect of true community belonging, true purpose and true spirituality is a fundamental reason for the extremely high rates of suicide and depression in our society. We are drowning in the modern demands of life and the human experience is not complete without a real sense of community and belonging. Consumption cannot be a replacement for these things. It does seem, however, that activities such as yoga or surfing, or any creative outlets that one can become passionate about, are ways to harmonize that side of the scale.

Hobbies you are passionate about can create identity and belonging but are also often viewed as luxuries or fringe activities that are only to be practiced in your spare time. That view needs to change. These interests should be promoted as priorities as they play a vital role in our overall health as humans, both mentally and physically. They also give us purpose and a sense of community and belonging, which are both primal human needs.

We live in a world where success is derived from our careers and work. When meeting new people, one of the most common questions is, "What do you do?" It is often asked within the first ten minutes of meeting someone. It seems to be such a defining question. What people are *really* asking is "What's your social status?" or "How successful are you?" or "How much money do you make?" I would love this question to be replaced by "What do you do for fun?" or "What do you do to make you feel like a kid again?" These questions would strike up much more of an authentic conversation about oneself. I would much rather talk about surfing, music, or art than explain that I stare at a computer all day entering data or whatever other mundane task we often do to make ends meet and survive.

Don't get me wrong. Some people have fulfilling careers that they are truly passionate about and identify with; it is their lifestyle. For most of us, though, our work is a smaller part of our lives. It is a means to play, to be alive, to provide, and to love. Because, at the end of the day, that is all surfing is. It is play time, it's being a kid again and soothing our spiritual side. The next time you meet new people, ask them what they do for fun. Watch their eyes light up as they talk about the hike they took in the forest, the picture they are painting, the song they are writing, or the river they recently kayaked. It creates a completely different dynamic.

Because of our status-driven society, people might tell you that the things you want to do can't be done. Most of the time those people mean well and are looking out for you. They don't want you to take risks because you might fail, but what they might not realize is that failing is good for you. Starting new challenges and being bad at something builds us into better beings. I have been told I can't do things my whole life, often by people who care about me. You can't move to America, you can't surf all the time, you can't live by the beach. Why not? Isn't it all about what I prioritize in life? If I want to live near the beach, I understand I will have to make sacrifices and pay much higher rent, but I will weigh that against the benefit of surfing every morning, being able to walk three minutes to the beach, and the sense of community found in my beach town. All those things make me a much happier and well-balanced person. I still go to work, but I am happier having surfed at 6 a.m. beforehand. If I am a happier person, then I am a better person for myself and others in my life.

What if society did treat both sides of the scale equally? Just because someone values the money they save living inland doesn't mean *I* have to. My value system promotes my mental health, balance, and, above all, my happiness, as well as how I treat others. Obviously, this value system needs to be balanced with responsibilities and commitments, but it is workable for me. This is not selfish, it's essential. Making time for the pursuit of pleasure is integral to a healthy life. Be a weekend warrior, go on the dawn raid before work, travel and surf tropical waves. Make it happen. Some people might say it is shallow or selfish to pursue a life of surfing, a life of passion, or whatever it is that gets your creative juices flowing. In the end, if I am happy, I can make others happy also. This is now highly evident in my friendships and relationships.

As surfers, we are extremely lucky to have something so fundamentally pure and exhilarating that it becomes easy to become passionate about and have a balanced scale. First and foremost, before all the consumption, media, and marketing, surfing is a sport—a physically demanding and technical activity. You need to train, learn, and practice. Then it becomes the lifestyle that, in turn, balances you and fuels your passion for the environment, for travel, for other people, for the natural world. It is an equalizer.

You can buy into the lifestyle as much as you want, but at the end of the day, it is important to remember that the lifestyle comes later, and the sport of surfing comes first—the practice, technique, and training. It should always be fun, but progression is a way to make it more fun. It took me a while to learn that, but once I did, it was of great benefit to my surfing.

Most humans need an identity. Psychologist Abraham Maslow defined a hierarchy of needs that included health, shelter, safety, esteem, and belonging. Belonging is an interesting one. As advanced as humans are, our primal instincts still dominate much of our thought patterns. We are very tribal, and we choose our tribes accordingly, politically, or ideologically. Just like our ancestors, we still believe there is safety in numbers. You can see this theory materialize everywhere today, whether in our extremely divided politics or on social media. The art of listening and debate has been marginalized, and tribal politics are in vogue. Most don't listen to understand, they listen to respond and rebuff opinions in defense of their tribe. Most are also of the impression that any other viewpoint or opinion other than their own needs to be suppressed and put down, again, in defense of their tribe's ideology. There is only room for *our* views and no one else's. This is basic tribal mentality, and it's understandable to an extent, because in evolutionary terms, the larger group will likely survive.

As surfers we have also joined a tribe; however, this tribe can be used for positivity and balance if we let it. There are many subcultures to surfing. There are longboarders, shortboarders, hipsters, hippies, punks, free surfers, professionals, and the old salty guys, to name a few. You can become whatever you want in surfing. You can even become an asshole if you so desire. Surfing can easily bring out the worst in you if you let it. You can get frustrated, angry, and annoyed with others. All the choices you make in and out of the water are yours and yours alone. If you are out taking all the waves, take a breather and let someone else take a wave. Just because you surf better and can catch more waves than everyone else doesn't mean you should. The choice is yours.

As I mentioned earlier, surfing can be very solitary at times. You can paddle out with friends, but when the wave takes you under, you are alone. Most of self-improvement comes from these solitary moments. When you are all alone, gliding along that green-blue face or spinning around underwater in a wipeout, and moments later the wave ceases to exist, it will be just you who got to experience that moment. Call me a hippy, but that's something quite special. Suddenly, a solitary act fulfills us, gives us identity, and fills us with confidence. Perhaps there is some other primal psychology at play, engaging so intimately with nature.

All you can do is find your truth, identity, and balance. Be honest with yourself and others and try to be a better person every day. Give back. Make a difference. Let surfing be the source of your positive attributes, not your selfish ones. If surfing becomes your lifestyle, use it for all the positives it brings.

THE STYLE TRAP

I often see grown men and women throwing temper tantrums while out in the water and just having an awful time. Don't get me wrong, being an average surfer can be very frustrating, we all cuss to ourselves while out in the lineup sometimes.

Chances are, as an average surfer, you have had some moments of brilliance in the water. You have probably surfed waves very well with style and grace, or maybe you surfed waves fast and aggressively, if that is more to your taste. Perhaps both? Whatever your style preference, we have all surfed waves well with great timing and flow. Those are the waves where everything clicks without even thinking about what we are doing technically. Often, this is because we let the wave dictate our surfing, rather than try to impose our will upon it.

For the average surfer, frustration stems from not being able to sustain that high level of performance every time we paddle out. Sometimes entire sessions are just plain frustrating. This all comes down to our mindset, approach, mentality, and, of course, time spent in the water.

Although surfing is a sport, we must remember what we are really doing out there. We are playing. Plain and simple. We are playing like kids in the ocean. We are riding fiberglass boards down slopes of water. Nothing more, nothing less. We work hard all week and have plenty of stressors on land with bills and responsibilities. Why would we make an escape an additional stressor? What we can gain from surfing is based on our own perspective and approach to the game.

It goes without saying that the lineup can be an intimidating setting. Whether you're braving the outside for the first time on your new fiberglass board or paddling out to the same old jetty close to home for the tenth year in a row, there seems to always be a stench of judgement in the air that invites feelings of insecurity. You better show everybody around you that you can surf. You better prove you belong to the tribe.

I remember various times in my earlier surfing days when I was utterly intimidated just sitting out back. I was so insecure about my skill set that I didn't think I belonged. Those types of thoughts and that type of insecurity can ruin a session instantly. Some days I would just sit there and not catch a single wave. Today, I can identify people who I think are feeling that same way. They will paddle for waves but hesitate and miss at the crucial moment, over and over again. Of course, there are also technique issues at play, but commitment, confidence, and attitude are imperative attributes to gain the skills needed to be a competent surfer.

I was twenty the first time I paddled out at Oceanside Pier. I had been in California for all of two days. Me and my buddy, Phil, went on a three-week road trip through California from San Diego to Santa Cruz and back. It was just two young guys from England, a rented red Pontiac, two backpacks, and our surfboards. We were two kooks with no plans other than to surf, explore, and have fun.

Phil is still my best friend to this day. I have known him for almost thirty years. He's a tall, skinny, blonde haired guy with tattoos and a never-ending smile. He is the type of friend who you don't see for a while, but when you sit down to catch up it's as if nothing has changed at all. He is always full of positivity and motivation to surf—motivation that is sometimes needed when my own is lacking. Phil is the perfect surf trip companion. He is easygoing, mellow, up for anything, perpetually stoked, and perpetually stoned.

It was a gorgeous, seventy-degree day in January when we pulled our conspicuously rented car, complete with Nevada license plates, up to the parking meter three blocks south of the Oceanside Pier. The waves were big. A strong off-season south swell was running and pushing head-high waves into the beach. This was a welcomed change as the waves up to that point had been knee high and onshore.

We paddled out next to the south side of the foreboding pier and sat out back with the pack. There were perhaps forty people out, mostly locals, including one large, tanned male who stood out due to his extremely loud and aggressive demeanor. He had tattoos on his face and kept sticking his middle finger up at the waves when he finished tearing them to pieces. He kept sitting next to me, or perhaps I was sitting next to him. Either way, he would catch all the best set waves and was getting tube rides on what I thought were unmakeable waves. These waves jacked up at the last minute and quickly ran off towards the shore. After ten minutes of being out amongst the madness, I was happy to watch. I had let my insecurities take hold and didn't want any waves anymore. I wasn't good enough to take waves from tattoo face, nor did I want a beating if I messed up. I would sit wider and pick off the scraps like the pathetic kook I thought I was.

Insecurity can be a strong emotion, and it seems to be rampant among some surfers. Back then, my insecurities would often lead me to what I used to call "the walk of shame." The walk of shame was the walk up the beach after I would paddle in from a session without getting any waves. I thought I would be partaking in the walk of shame that day in Oceanside. Phil was sitting fifty yards south of me, trying to catch a few straggling waves. He was mostly getting smashed and ground up, but at least he was trying. I saw him make one, and he made it look easy. What was wrong with me? I paddled half-heartedly for a few but obviously pulled out before going. My next move was to paddle down towards Phil. I thought maybe I could get some waves where it was a little less crowded. The self-deprecating thoughts began. *Come on Simon, get it together, you twat!*

The man with the tattoos had just taken the first wave of a solid, head-high set and was paddling back towards me when he shouted something at me that was unintelligible. I felt a little hot and nervous as I looked his way. *Oh shit, what did he say? Did I do something wrong?* He yelled again, "Lining up for you, pal!" I looked over my shoulder to see a beautiful wave lining up, and I was in pole position. It looked like the biggest wave of the session so far. The green water darkened as it approached. The wave rose up, and my stomach sank. I had more than enough ability at that time to surf the wave competently, but my insecurities had paddled out with me, and my confidence was lacking. A few whistles went up from the crowd. I knew everyone was watching. *Fuck, better take this beating like a man!* I pointed my board towards the beach at a slight angle and started to paddle. The wave started building and lifted me up. I must have angled my board perfectly because the shoulder guided me up, and the wave wasn't too steep or too soft. I jumped to my feet and cruised off to the bottom of the wave. The takeoff was easy, and as I shot off down the line, the view from the bottom of the wave was that of which every surfer loves to see—a long, head-high wall curving towards the beach. I placed my left hand in the wall, looked up at my next target, and headed back up towards the top of the wave. My board was speeding. I reached the top in a split second and hit my target as the section began to break. Back down I went as the wave continued to build in front of me. I was accelerating as fast as I could. Another section of inviting glassy water rose in front of me, and I obliged nature's invitation with another soft sweeping arc to the top and back down. The feeling was amazing. I was oozing with confidence. I turned to cut back towards the pocket when my board stopped halfway through the turn, and my body continued. I wiped out with a smile as my face penetrated the water, and the lights were turned off. *Damn.* I had bogged my rail and fallen during the turn. Still, it was a good wave, a really good wave.

As I floated in the water while I watched the wave head off towards the beach, I did what any self-respecting surfer would do in that moment. I turned my board over and inspected my fins to see what had caused me to fall. I knew damn well my fins were completely fine, but I had to blame something, everyone was watching. At least I thought they were.

I owe that angry man with the tattooed face a beer. The confidence I gained from this one wave made surfing during the rest of my trip far more enjoyable. I often think surfing is fifty percent physical and fifty percent psychological. I can have a terrible session if I get inside my own head with negative thoughts. It often only takes one good wave to change everything and boost my confidence.

There are certain characters in every lineup, no matter where you surf in the world. There will come a day when you'll be in the lineup with a tattoo face or maybe the old guy on his 10-foot tanker who constantly takes waves from way out back and begins trimming in a straight line to the inside with a look of glory on his face. If he's not there, you'll most likely see a chatterbox. You know, *that* guy. He starts by asking the time and then remarks how the waves are a bit fat and slow for their liking today. The next thing you know, he's reciting daily experiences from last year's trip to Costa Rica. *We all love surf stories, mate, but not when I'm trying to find my ocean zen.* Then, of course, there are the stone-faced locals. These are the ones that get the best waves and pull a crazy air reverse on the inside. They don't say much but let their surfing do the talking, saying the same thing again and again.

What about the rest of the lineup? What about the average surfers like you and me? What about the ones who are caught in what I call the style trap? You know who you are. You probably catch about three of the ten waves you attempt in a session. The other waves are missed from hesitation. You get hung up in the lip, fall over the back, slap the water, and mumble something about wave quality before paddling five yards back to the takeoff zone. I know because this was me for a long, long time. I was stuck in the style trap for at least eight years.

The style trap is the plateau I mentioned earlier. Almost every surfer gets there and remains there for some time or maybe even forever. The enlightenment I gained from learning of the style trap released me from the plateau, and I began progressing in my surfing for the first time in years. I surf better now at thirty-three than at twenty-three—sometimes.

If you look at most lineups, most of the surfers are distinctly average due to lack of progression. Sure, the lineup can look busy and intimidating, but is it? Let's look at it and use some logic. In most regular beach break lineups, there might be five surfers who genuinely surf at an expert or elite level. There are typically a couple of obvious beginners out there as well. The other 80% of surfers are your average Joes.

There's nothing wrong with being an average Joe, after all, that is why I wrote this book. The problems come when average surfers are caught in the style trap. Those stuck in the style trap are afraid to look bad, afraid to fall, and afraid to fail, and they get frustrated when they do. They look like steely, good surfers, sitting and paddling around the lineup with confidence, hunting down peaks. On the handful of waves they get, you'll see a few bottom to top turns. They look like they're in control. The problem is, there is no longer progression in their surfing. Self-awareness and insecurity have taken over, even though they are surfing quite competently with limited confidence. These surfers are both insecure and confident. They are confident with performing the same two turns they have practiced for ten years but insecure about looking bad.

Remember when you started surfing? How fun was it? Remember paddling in, fumbling to your feet, and falling with a flourish? Remember trying to turn your board for the first time and eating it? Remember all the wipeouts? Remember the two-foot wave that felt like a double overhead pipe bomb? It was so fun being a beginner when surfing was all about progression and goals. Then you started to get better.

Your progression took time, but it was steady. You were trying so hard and falling a lot. Suddenly, you could drop in, trim the line, and even link a bottom and top turn that didn't look too shabby. After kicking out, you'd paddle back out to the lineup feeling like you were on top of the world. Maybe you snagged one or two more like that in a session. You reached a level of comfort out in the blue. It may have taken months or years, but you were finally no longer a beginner in the lineup. You belonged to the tribe. But, why is it that a few years later you're still surfing at that exact same level? It's because you're in the style trap. You've hit the plateau.

When you started surfing, everyone knew you were a beginner. No matter how much you tried to hide it, everyone could tell. It was obvious when you paddled out with your arms and legs flailing, when the nose of your board was pointing up while paddling, or when you fell off your board while trying to sit upright and stare at the horizon with everyone else. The difference was that everyone accepted your role, including you. No one cared if you fell. Even you didn't care. It was fun, remember? There is an old saying that if you are not falling off, you are not trying hard enough. It's very true, and not just as a beginner. You should always be falling, wiping out, and trying to progress. No one is going to get it right on the first try. You should start to enjoy wiping out again; see it as part of surfing and your progression. Why should things be different now, because you can put a few turns together? You can look at those beginners and take waves from them? You can hold your own in the lineup and impress your friends? Congratulations, you pass the judgement test. You belong, best not fall in front of the crowd. But, the truth is: no one else *really* cares how you surf. Sure, if you catch a good one, we notice. We might even tell you. But if you wipeout or fall, we might smile and laugh because wipeouts are funny. We don't really care otherwise about anyone else's surfing. Good for you for going for it, that is what most of us are really thinking.

It is time to drop our insecurities and just surf. Release yourself from the style trap and stop caring what others are thinking. Start progressing again. Don't do that same bottom to top trim combo. Try a cut back. Try a floater. Hell, try and boost an air, if you want. Try to enjoy surfing again. We all started surfing because it was fun. Then the challenge hooked us. We wanted to get better. That's the best part—challenging yourself to get better. Teach yourself new moves, fall, smile, wipeout, and then get up and do it again. Stop being complacent. Complacency is boring and frustrating. Progress by actually trying. It's that easy.

Of course, you will also want to maximize your wave count and enjoy surfing every wave. If you are falling all the time, then perhaps it won't be all that fun. That is where drills can help you improve. To do this, you'll need to wear a watch in the water. I know that goes against the free spirit and essence of surfing, but sometimes functionality counts. The next time you are out surfing, wear a watch and break your surf session into twenty-minute intervals. The first twenty minutes can be time spent catching waves and surfing comfortably, if you wish. Get comfortable in the lineup and show that you belong. For the second set of twenty minutes, set a new goal, a challenge that will probably lead to falling. Cutbacks and floaters are good exercises to try. Repeat and practice for the whole twenty-minute timeframe. You shouldn't go into this blindly, obviously. Coaching or research on how to actually pull off the maneuver will help you. But, remember, every time you fall you are subconsciously learning, and your muscles and brain are remembering and assessing for the next time. After the second set of twenty minutes, move on to the next challenge. I often finish with another free surf, just for fun. Technique and maneuvers are obviously fundamental to this type of progression. Once you know how to trim, top turn, and bottom turn, you should be learning cutbacks and floaters.

Knowing where the speed and power are in a wave is crucial. But the most common mistake I see in surfing is the take-off. The take-off is ground zero. If you find yourself constantly nose diving or missing waves, there are two simple errors that are usually responsible: speed and the position of your board's nose. You'll hear many surf instructors talking about prone body positioning when you are catching waves. They may tell you that you are too far forward and causing the board to nose dive. As a beginner, when you are first learning this may well be true, but as an intermediate, average surfer, this is most likely not the case at all. The main reason one will miss a wave or a surfboard will nosedive is because of the angle and speed of the wave. When a wave begins to break, it is at its steepest and fastest point. If your board is meandering at the top of the wave because you are consciously or subconsciously hesitating or paddling too slowly, you will not make the drop. The best-case scenario is that you will just fall off the back of the wave. The worst-case scenario is that you will be going headfirst into the ocean floor.

The two fundamental ways of fixing these errors are paddle speed and board positioning. You must paddle faster and harder with no hesitation. Once you decide to go on a wave, go! When your subconscious tells you to stop because you might fall or get hurt, that is the time to paddle as hard as you can and get yourself down the wave face, away from the top. Secondly, leave as little daylight as possible between the nose of your board and the water without sinking it. Concentrate on these fundamentals and see if your wave count improves. Next time you are in the lineup, watch how many average surfers miss waves. I can almost guarantee that the next person you see who misses a wave at the crucial moment will have their board nose pointing straight out or upwards at the critical take-off point. Remember, make sure the nose is lower than the tail on take-off.

Lastly, don't hesitate, just go. I no longer do the walk of shame because I have a rule that if I haven't caught a wave within twenty minutes, I will go on the next wave, even if it's closing out. Sometimes you need a good wipeout to wake you up.

What about board selection? We are lucky in this day and age that almost any board is acceptable within reason. When I began learning, shortboards were the accepted norm, and longboards were okay, if that was your thing. Nowadays, you can ride whatever you want without too many judging stares or comments.

My first board, aside from the foam tops we rented from the Little Pink Surf Shop in Croyde, was a borrowed 5'8 fish. This was no ordinary fish, it was circa 1980, made from some type of heavy plastic, and about five inches thick all the way through. The board was white with bright green and yellow lines on it. I don't remember the manufacturer, but I was told it was a factory molded pop out, whatever that meant. It looked like it had more in common with a windsurf board than a surfboard. I was fifteen, and I didn't care. It was short, and I thought I looked cool, but what did I know? That was yet another short board that probably halted my progression for a substantial amount of time.

I borrowed the board from my friend Adam's stepfather, Oz. he had moved to our village from England's surfing capital, Newquay, a few years prior to the start of my surfing life. The stories of his days shredding big waves in the West Country were legendary to us youngsters. I was stoked that a real Newquay surfer had leant me a board.

I look at younger surfers these days with all the latest and greatest kits and can't help but feel like they are missing out on something. A right of passage, in some sense. In those first months of our surfing lives, all our equipment was borrowed. Thinking back, we must have looked like the biggest group of kooks on the planet. I was wearing my stepfather's aged wetsuit from the eighties. It was a faded luminous green and purple and at least seven millimeters thick. My buddy, Nick, used to wear his dad's summer diving wetsuit with luminous yellow removable arms that would zip on and off. We'd also wear board shorts over our wetsuits. What were we thinking?

It just goes to prove my point with the style trap. We accepted our roles as beginners, we had no insecurities, and we progressed past those days. We didn't take our surfing as seriously and loved every minute of it. Like any teenager, there was always a bit of self-consciousness in the air, but we really just wanted to surf, have fun, and get better.

I now try to do my best not to fall into the style trap. I ride boards that are fun and suit my style of surfing. Since those early days, I have not owned a conventional shortboard. I ride funboards, eggs, twin fins, and progressive fun designs. Catching waves, having fun, and progressing are my surfing priorities.

My friends and I continued to progress after those early years in borrowed wetsuits. With progression came confidence, with confidence came bigger waves, and with bigger waves came bigger consequences and challenges. For me, the biggest of all those new challenges was fear.

FEAR

I was about eighteen years old when I experienced my first terrifying wipeout—the one where you think you might die. I had experienced wipeouts before and had gone over the falls a lot, but this was different.

I was surfing in North Devon at a beach called Croyde Bay. I had been surfing for a few years at the time and began to progress quite quickly. My skills and technique were getting better, and my confidence was high. That had a lot to do with the competitive nature of my friends. We were all progressing at a fast pace because we all wanted to be the best. I had never really been good at anything before. I was decent at a lot of things, but there were always others in my group of friends who were better. Surfing was the first thing I did that made me one of the most talented in my group of friends. I was progressing at a faster rate than others. From that moment on, I was content with being a bad skateboarder and a half-decent guitarist, but I was definitely going to be a good surfer.

It wasn't a nasty competitiveness but more of a rivalry between friends that went unspoken. We would swap places in the ranks too. Some days I would surf better by making the biggest wave or performing a better turn, and other days my friends were better. It was very healthy, in terms of progression, for all of us.

One of the main things I kept quiet at that time was that I couldn't swim very well. I learned to surf before I learned to swim. When you're eighteen, and all your friends are doing something, you don't want to be left behind. You do what it takes, even if it might kill you. Logic comes later.

My friend, Nick, was easily my closest competition at the time. Nick was my childhood friend and original surfing companion. We grew up together in a small fishing village on the south coast. Nick was a short and stocky blonde with a passing resemblance to pro surfer Mick Fanning, if you squinted in the dark. He was a talented surfer and a great guy with dark, edgy humor and bright energy. He inspired me to improve and progress in surfing. To this day, we have a friendly rivalry in the water.

The thing about Nick was that he loved bigger waves. When I say bigger, I am talking about English standards, so that means above head-high, maybe a couple of feet overhead on those rare days. The day of my first truly terrifying wipeout was one of those rare days. It was low tide and way overhead. The sky was black, and thunder clouds were on the horizon, but you take what you can get in England.

When it is not closing out, Croyde can be a great wave. In the summer you could be forgiven for thinking it's a beginner's wave. Some days, at high tide, it can be a good wave to learn on, especially if it's in the knee-high range. However, on this day it wasn't. It was big, dark, powerful, and menacing—a steep, fast, and hollow beast that was breaking hard on to the shallow, low tide sand bar.

As Nick and I watched from the parking lot beforehand, he looked excited and eager to get in the black soup. He was always like that on big days. I often wondered if he was genuine or if he knew that I was nervous and was winding me up. As we changed into our wetsuits, we would yell things at each other like, "Time for a beat down, son!" or "Daddy's angry today!" Yes, we were a little weird. I was excited in these moments, but to be completely honest, I was more scared than eager.

We walked across the street from the Downend car park, a dusty lot with an incredible view of the sand dune surrounded beach, located at the entrance to the ancient village of Croyde. We pulled on our wetsuit hoods and headed down a narrow pathway that ran between two bramble bushes towards the beach. Those type of days always made the walk seem a lot shorter. As our seven-millimeter neoprene and rubber boots crunched on the chalk and rocks, my stomach felt like it was in my throat. We could see a huge set coming in on the horizon, and we both began to hoot and holler. I couldn't help but think I was celebrating my own imminent death. The walk led us down a small coastal path towards the west end of the beach and large rocky outcrop. We passed a family walking their dog. They were warmly wrapped in coats and scarves and gave us a fated smile as they wished us luck. I felt like a warrior heading to war. The chances of my return were faint.

I was confident in my surfing at the time but not for conditions like the ones presenting themselves that day. The next set we saw seemed like it had a twelve-foot face. The wave at low tide in Croyde is a beast when it's big. It has a fast take-off and a short, heavy barrel section. There were no more than six surfers out that day. It was serious.

Nick always paddled out first. No matter the conditions, he had a thing about running off down the beach and paddling out before anyone else. As we approached my fate, he was gone, and I was left putting my leash on at the water's edge. Did I mention I was riding a round nose fish? My chances of surviving that day were slender, at best. I paddled out and somehow made it through to the outside with just a few duck dives due to a massive lull in the sets. The currents and riptides were relentless but were assisting to ease the paddle out. I was out back in no time sitting next to Nick. He was a little quieter now that we were out amongst the monsters. We sat for what I'm sure seemed a lot longer than it really was before we saw the first shadow appear on the calm horizon. It was approaching fast. I had never seen a wave that big in real life. I felt helpless as it approached. "Go on then, son, *your* wave," I said to

Nick as I turned and paddled toward safety. Nick began to scratch and paddle towards the beach. He was going. The wave was upon us, and Nick was gone over the ledge like a paratrooper. I, on the other hand, was paddling up and over the back of the wave. I do love that feeling, even to this day. The feeling when you paddle over a big swell line and drop down the other side to safety. There is something about it, maybe the primal instinct of survival. It is even better when you are paddling over it with other surfers, and they don't make it, but you do. Everyone must pay their dues. There is a sadistic pleasure in seeing your friends dragged to the bottom of the ocean, or maybe that's   just   me.

The first wave passed, and I looked back and saw Nick's luminous yellow board tombstoning as he came up for air. He looked a little shaken and was yelling something that I couldn't make out. He began to point at the horizon behind me. I turned and saw another wave approaching. This one was an absolute behemoth. It was getting bigger and darker as it approached. I was way out of my depth. *It's okay*, I thought, *just keep heading for the horizon, and sit out in the safe zone.* I didn't have to ride any of those things, just survive. It was about five feet before the wave hit me that I experienced that hot sense of panic and realized I was completely fucked. The thing was massive. It had at least a ten-foot face. I was paddling, trying desperately to get out behind it to the relative safety of the open ocean, away from the impact zone. I was about halfway up the face, and I was stranded. As it began to break, I knew I was going with it. I stayed on my board and closed my eyes. As I held my breath, it happened.

At first, it was quiet and strangely peaceful, like I was floating backwards through the air. I wasn't. I was going backwards, headfirst and upside down on my board in the lip of a ten-foot wave. As I penetrated the water it was like getting hit by a big rig from two directions. Then the floating feeling happened again. Somehow, I was going up over the waterfall again, this time underwater. This time I got pushed down, *hard*. It was absolute mayhem and violence. I was tumbling every which way like a pair of sneakers thudding around in a washing machine. It was pitch dark, and I didn't know which way was up. The force and power of the turbulence was like nothing else I have felt, but that wasn't the worst part. The worst part was feeling powerless. Panic started to set in. *How long is this going to last? I can't hold my breath much longer. I can't really swim.* At least I had my board to help me float. As the terror began to end, I started crawling and scratching for the surface only to hit the ocean floor. I was swimming the wrong way. I was so disoriented. I turned around and made it to the surface. The brightness hit me like someone had switched on a light in the middle of the night, waking me up. Then I felt excruciating pain in my inner right thigh. I looked down to see a palm-sized tear in my suit. I later came to the conclusion that at some point my board hit me fin-first and cut my leg. My leg was bruised for weeks. I pulled on the leash of my board only to feel no weight. The leash had snapped, and the board was gone. Panic began to set in again. I had to get to the beach. I looked up and saw Nick in the shallows, making a dash towards the beach. He had taken a fair beating himself and was heading for dry land. I turned the other direction to see another monstrous wave crashing about fifteen yards behind me. *Time to learn to swim.* Figuring that swimming was like paddling but without the board, I somehow made it to the beach. I think the waves did most of the work by washing me ashore like driftwood.

In some respects, I was lucky that day. I think every surfer can tell a similar story. We've all had that horrific wipeout. In fact, I have had numerous in the years since. It comes down to how one processes those experiences. Terrifying wipeouts can help or hinder your surfing, depending on how you look at them. Even when we feel somewhat experienced and comfortable in the ocean, our most terrifying and humbling wipeout could be just around the corner.

As Nick and I walked back up the beach that day, we didn't feel humiliated or ashamed. We felt gratified with a sense of perseverance. We lost the battle but we would win the war. We would learn from that defeat and return to fight another day. Fear had turned to fuel.

Fear plays a part in dictating the way people surf. Whether you are a beginner or Kelly Slater, everyone gets scared out there. Let's not forget that the ocean is the dominant force in our world. She has moods; she can be friendly, playful, grumpy, or angry. Her mood can change in an instant, and we should never underestimate   her.

I feel more comfortable in larger surf than I did years ago. This is simply due to experience. I experienced progressive, big surf and learned to accept and even enjoy wipeouts. Due to injuries, I learned over time to get as far away from my board as possible. With practice, I learned that I can hold my breath way longer than fifteen seconds. Most importantly, I learned not to panic. Panic is our enemy. I have heard of and learned of many techniques over the years on how to relax amongst chaos. I, personally, like to count or sing in my head.

Every surfer has similar emotions and fears during a session. Each person may experience a different level of emotion, but the emotion of one surfer is likely very similar to the next. The beginner can feel the exact same emotion on a two-foot wave as the pro surfer charging at ten-foot pipeline. The only thing separating the two is tolerance level and set limitations. When you first start paddling out as a beginner, a two-foot wave can be intimidating. Fear is only due to the unknown. Once you experience enough two-foot waves, they become fun and are no longer scary. Next, three or four-foot waves become intimidating until you conquer them, and so forth. It does get a little harder to continue to conquer bigger waves as they are less common, depending on where you are located. In the end, consistent progression is the key to conquering your fears. Get out there, be smart, and push your limits.

WATER

Surfing is incredible in so many ways. It gives us so much. The feeling of riding waves, being one with nature, and having the main arena for our pastime located in some of the most beautiful places on earth is a nice return on investment. Watch surfers coming out of the water on any given Sunday, and you will likely see them smiling, bursting with contentment and self-confidence.

Surfing is a lifelong journey and commitment. It takes a special kind of human to reach a competent skill level as a surfer. You must give hours of time to the ocean, month after month, year after year. Even after little progression, we blindly return to the water each week, constantly being slapped around like a rag doll and humbled by Mother Nature. Yet, we persevere, and it soon becomes the one constant in life.

Having a partner that understands that surfing is a true passion and character enhancer is important. I run into a lot of surfers who have partners, both male and female, who share that their partners do not fully understand what surfing is to them. Their partners think they are just playing around when there are much more important things that need tending to on the weekend. Essentially, as I mentioned, we are just playing, but it is also something much deeper than that. Surfing makes us stronger, it satisfies our spiritual side, the side that is most neglected and relegated in modern society.

Surfing has a stigma that other hobbies don't. It doesn't quite fit into a clean category. Yes, it's a sport, but one can argue that it is different than playing in the amateur softball or football league on a Friday night. It's also a hobby, but it's not quite an art like painting, music, or photography. It demands so much more than any of these things. It demands our entire lives, but it also gives us way more in return. Perhaps the time demanded by surfing is one of the reasons some partners find it hard to accept. The return on investment with surfing is largely internal and not outwardly evident to others.

Many non-surfing partners see surfing as an immature, meaningless activity that offers no more than some fun in the water. It is likely the same partner that would give more credibility to a more mainstream activity. To be able to clearly articulate what surfing means to us, we need to truly understand what surfing *does* for us.

Sometimes, I still find it a little embarrassing to talk about surfing to people who are not surfers. As a thirty-three-year-old man, when my colleagues share their weekend doings on Monday morning, I can't help but assume they think I'm immature for surfing all the time. It's also hard to express the activity itself. On Saturday morning, I was dropping into overhead bombs and grabbing rail like my life depended on it. On Monday morning, I was explaining this to the office receptionist who was staring at me as if I was speaking a different language. Perhaps I was. After all, there is no real sporting objective to surfing. There is no goal to score or hoop to shoot at, no time limit, and no one to beat, at least not in the average surfer's world.

I consider myself lucky to have a better half who understands my addiction and has her own separate love affair with the mistress that is surfing. My better half is Steph. She is a fascinating, alluring, beautiful woman. She is half Hispanic and half Filipino with a head of long, wavy, thick, brown hair. She has dark skin and an athletic build. She is a natural beauty but is completely unaware of it. She has an innate humbleness, almost shyness about her. That shyness disappears when it comes to her passion for surfing or anything adventurous or outdoors.

One cloudy and cool day in April, I was driving back from a surf session at San Onofre with Steph. We both had incredibly difficult weeks with work and general life stressors. Getting away to the ocean together has always been the remedy to a bad week. We had surfed for three hours in waves that were waist-high and slightly onshore. The conditions weren't great, but it was something to soothe us. It was one of those days where the sun wouldn't quite come out from behind the clouds. There was a slight promise of summer, but grayness lingered in the sky like a shadow. The water was also unseasonably cold. Regardless of the environmental conditions, we were destined to have a good day. After all, we *were* surfing. After a fun day of catching waves on our mid-length boards, we drove north on the 5 freeway to head back to Huntington Beach, chatting and laughing as usual. Everything felt the same as any other adventurous day trip. The cars were whizzing past the freeway with families going about their Sunday business. That day, though, there was an added aura of gratitude to surfing that was in the air. The stressful week we experienced and the fact that we had not surfed together for some time led itself to a blissful, surfed out feeling that escorted us home in the truck cab that day—that feeling where your shoulders ache, your hair is thick, your eyes are salty, and your spirit is satisfied. That is one circumstance where the cliché rings true: "only a surfer knows the feeling." And it is a great feeling to know.

Steph said something to me on that drive that made me think long and hard. It was something that I had heard before but had taken for granted. She explained that she was trying to change some things about herself for the better. She was trying to live a little more in the moment and worry less about the future or past. This is something that we had discussed before. As partners, we often discuss and contemplate subjects on self-awareness and improvement as we are always striving to improve both as individuals and as a couple. I think it is so important to remain individuals in a relationship. It makes no sense to me how common it is for couples to become one complete entity. We all start as unique individuals, it's what attracts us to one another. Then, for some reason, a lot of couples become one. They are always together and possessive of each other's time. Steph and I love spending time together. We especially enjoy surfing and hiking together, but we also do things separately and enjoy our own interests. It keeps us strong as individuals and interesting to one another. In the long run, two strong individuals make a stronger couple.

One of my highest held values in life is awareness and learning to have a realistic perception of one's own self, including all negative traits. Nobody's perfect, but if we are aware, conscious, accountable, and willing to accept and appreciate ourselves, including the negatives, we can continue to adapt, evolve, and become better people on our respective journeys. This is something that we need to work on daily. Sometimes we need to be humble enough to be shown by another where we can improve. Sometimes our actions and choices lead us to depths and dark places within ourselves, where self-awareness and change is the only option left. Either way, once you begin the practice of self-improvement, life becomes more fulfilling for one as an individual as well as for those who surround us.

As we progressed on our Sunday drive, Steph continued explaining her plans as we sailed northbound past the Orange County suburbs with the other weekend traffic. She told me that surfing is one of the only things in life where she doesn't think about the future or past or stress or worry about things while she is doing it. The only thing that matters when she surfs is surfing—the next wave, the joy, and the challenge. This was something I had also heard from others and something I had probably stated myself. However, I had never really contemplated what it actually meant.

When any surfer paddles out into the water, they surrender completely to a higher power. The ocean is a vast, expansive body of living and breathing nature. We are nothing in comparison, just a microorganism. The ocean can do as she pleases with us. She doesn't care about human advancement or technology. She doesn't care about our weapons, possessions, structures, or egos. She is the mightiest of forces on the planet. She is beautiful, powerful, and deadly.

As surfers, our attitudes towards the ocean should not be one of conquest or with a mind to challenge her. We should respect her and let her challenge us to work with her. If we surf a good wave, we have not succeeded through force, we have been *allowed* to succeed. When we leave the ocean after a surf session, whether we have surfed well or not, we have survived the water.

Biologist and author Wallace J. Nichols said, "*Across all spiritual traditions, cultures, and times, you find the use of water to achieve states of awe, grace, and love. We scientists avoid those words like the plague. But if you're on the water a lot, those end up being the words you need to describe your experiences.*"

We know that water is the lifeblood of the planet and our very existence. We also know that water is soothing and healing. "Flow state" is the psychological term for when people are fully engrossed in what they're doing at that moment. Many activities can put one into a flow state of mind; surfing, however, has some extra added physiological benefits, due, in part, to the mammalian dive reflex. The mammalian dive reflex is the physiological effect of cool or cold water on the human body. When our face enters any body of water that has a temperature that is cooler than the surrounding air, our bodies have an extreme reaction.

In 1962, a Swedish-born researcher named Per Scholander gathered a team of volunteers, covered them with electrodes to measure their heart rates, and poked them with needles to draw blood. Scholander had seen the biological functions of seals reverse in deep water. The seals, he wrote, actually seemed to gain oxygen the longer and deeper they dove. Scholander wondered if water could trigger this effect in humans.

Scholander started the experiment by leading volunteers into an enormous water tank and monitoring their heart rates as they dove to the bottom of the tank. Water triggered an immediate decrease in heart rate. Next, Scholander told the volunteers to hold their breath, dive down, strap themselves into an array of fitness equipment submerged at the bottom of the tank, and do a short, vigorous workout. In all cases, no matter how hard the volunteers exercised, their heart rates still plummeted.

On land, exercise greatly increases heart rate. The volunteers' slower heart rates meant that they used less oxygen and therefore could stay underwater longer. Water has a powerful capacity to slow our hearts. Scholander noticed something else. Once his volunteers were underwater, the blood in their bodies began flooding away from their limbs and toward their vital organs. He'd seen the same thing happen in deep-diving seals decades earlier. By shunting blood away from less important areas of the body, the seals were able to keep organs like the brain and heart oxygenated longer, extending the amount of time they could stay submerged. Immersion in water triggered the same biological response in humans, meaning, in an evolutionary sense, we humans are built for water. We are not only built for water but built to be in water for prolonged periods of time. Perhaps this is a reason why we feel so relaxed in water, provided we have an ability to swim and remain   calm.

There are numerous other reasons why surfing can make us feel fully focused, relaxed, and free from stress. Although technology is slowly encroaching into the lineup with Apple watches, GoPros, and even phones, we are still relatively distraction-free while surfing. When we surf we can do so without the interruption of cell phones, traffic, written language, and any need for communication at all. Even when we paddle out with friends we surf alone most of the time. Solitude and isolation can be especially good for human healing and development. Although we are tribal by nature, we can benefit from being alone. Surfing gives us those benefits of solitude without the negatives, such as pain or prolonged loneliness.

I work five days a week. I have bills, rent, a partner, three dogs, and a business. I have had times in my life where I have worked two jobs. I have had times where I was distracted, stressed, depressed, and neglectful of myself—of my health and spirituality. Surfing was always there, either predominantly or in the background, nagging, deep down inside, reminding me that there was a cure, and not just a cure but an equalizer, a balance, a reminder of how to live correctly on land by being at sea. Surfing has the ability to calm me enough to see problems clearly and lessen my anxiety or confusion. It is the great equalizer. In the end, I have never come from a surf session feeling more stressed than before I paddled out. If you truly love surfing, if it is truly in your blood and soul, then it calls you like an addiction.

So, why am I not addicted to other hobbies I have? I love football, or soccer for the American reader. Since the age of five I have been a die-hard Tottenham Hotspur fan. Spurs, as they are affectionately known, are a football club from North London. I grew up playing footy every day of my life. Every afternoon after school, from the ages of five through fifteen, I could be found kicking a ball against my back fence or with friends playing a pickup match in the park. I played for my school teams and still love to kick a ball around today. Most weekends I get up at 6 a.m. and drive to the British pub in Orange County to watch Spurs play live on English time with 100 other nutters. I love the game.

I also love music. I learned to play the guitar when I was nine years old. I have played music most of my life, joining bands and recording songs. I have a vast record collection, albeit in digital format these days. I can get lost for hours playing guitar, writing music, or listening to a couple of albums. We might have numerous passions, but why don't these other things influence our lives like surfing? Surfing took over my life both consciously and subconsciously. Surfing transcended everything. It got into my mind, my veins, and my blood. Surfing has been a priority in my life for almost twenty years. It made me an addict.

But what does that mean? What is an addiction? According to a popular definition:

"Addiction is a condition in which a person engages in use of a substance or in a behavior for which the rewarding effects provide a compelling incentive to repeatedly pursue the behavior despite detrimental consequences. Addiction may involve the use of substances such as alcohol, inhalants, opioids, cocaine, nicotine, and others, or behaviors such as gambling; there is scientific evidence that the addictive substances and behaviors share a key neurobiological feature—they intensely activate brain pathways of reward and reinforcement, many of which involve the neurotransmitter dopamine."

So, do we all have a surfing addiction? It sounds paradoxical because, as stated, the word "addiction" is tied to detrimental consequences. Does surfing have detrimental consequences? Most certainly, yes, both on land and in the ocean. A detrimental consequence could be having a partner break up with you because you spend too much time in the water doing something that they don't fully understand. It could also show in the selfishness of the activity. We don't want to share waves, and we get mad when someone drops in on us. Even worse, the consequence could be getting slammed on to a shallow reef and sustaining a serious injury or even meeting death. There are definitely consequences to what we do. But, unlike most addictions, surfing has bountiful positive outcomes too. The effects of surfing can be quite positive if we channel the right approaches and philosophies towards the lifestyle and activity.

Somewhat recently, I was surfing on the north side of the pier in Huntington Beach. The waves were about waist-high, the wind was cross shore, and I was not surfing well. After falling on my first wave of the day, I got inside my head with negative thoughts, which often has a way of ruining my session.

After about ten minutes, I pulled into a little right that stayed open for me, and off down the line I went. It wasn't anything special, but the wave was satisfying enough. I neared the end of my ride and eased into a cutback only to notice a guy cruising along behind me the whole time. I remembered seeing him when I paddled for the wave but thought he hadn't made it. I had clearly dropped in on him and surfed (almost) the entire wave blissfully unaware. *Damn*, I felt like a moron. I've surfed for years, and just like the rest of us, I occasionally drop in on people by accident.

Sometimes they drop in on me too, and I might get a little mad inside when they do. But, I try to practice kindness and keep a positive outlook.

The guy I'd just dropped in on did a great job of the latter. I paddled back out and apologized. "No worries, brother," he said, "I was trying to synchronize with your turns." He laughed and paddled off. I laughed. The next good set wave came in, and even though I was in a good position, I left it to him, and he obliged. This kind of scene repeats around the world daily, even when surfing seems to bring out the worst in us and our selfish ways. Self-awareness is a great tool to have in surfing and in life. We must always remember that compassion has no limit, and kindness has no enemy. Let surfing teach and bring out the best in us, not the worst.

We can all relate to the cliché saying, "Only a surfer knows the feeling." If that phrase is talking about the act of riding the wave, then that feeling that only we know is triggered by the release of some "happiness hormones," such as dopamine, serotonin, and endorphins. These chemicals have mood-altering effects and are known to be habit-forming.

Good waves are the source of intense joy for a surfer. We want to relive those feelings over and over again. Those same waves can also turn to terror in an instant. We live and experience some of the best and worst moments of our lives out in the ocean. I have experienced astounding joy and overwhelming horror, panic, and dread. Yet, time and time again, I will paddle back out. Maybe one day I will meet the detrimental consequence of my addiction in the ocean. There are not many other sports or activities people partake in on a Sunday morning that could offer serious injury or death as part of the game.

There are also negative consequences that manifest within our personalities. It is all too easy for us to let selfishness and ego rule when we are surfing. Much like an addict, we forget to be compassionate and giving when we are out looking for our fix of water. We want the next ride, we want the secret spot to ourselves, and we don't want anyone ruining our session or stealing waves from us. Maybe that's why surfing transcends like nothing else. Maybe it is literally so stimulating to our brains that it becomes a chemical addiction.

The truth is, I can't tell you why surfing holds such a powerful force over so many, but I know I could fill the pages of this book one hundred times over with real stories of people whose lives have been changed by surfing. There are people who have had spiritual and metaphysical experiences when surfing entered into their lives, people who have ended relationships for surfing, people who have stolen for surfing, people who have cried for surfing, and people who have become better humans through surfing.

I have also heard people say that surfing is no different from any other passion. Some people live for golf. Does golf demand as much from a person as surfing? It could be argued that it delivers the same reward. What if that is true? What if surfing is nothing more than a fun activity, and surfers are such a neurotic bunch that we try to attach a meaning to it so that we can justify the amount of time we spend doing it, talking about it, writing about it, or dreaming about it. I don't believe that golf holds the same mystique and power over a person as surfing. When we paddle out, whether it is at our usual spot or a new discovery, we surrender to the uncertainty of nature and ourselves. Are the waves going to be good? Am I going to surf well? Will I get hurt? That uncertainty is a good thing as it humbles the egos we have little control of. Do golfers feel those same feelings when they walk onto a golf course? Perhaps, but I doubt it.

Me at 16 with my borrowed 8-foot Superfrog. Devon, England 2001

Some of the original weekend warriors drinking cider. (Left to right: Nick, Phil, Me, Ben, and Borris) England, 2004

Headed to Cornwall for the weekend. I'm stoked about my borrowed plastic fish board. Dorset, England, 2003

Boris and Phil. Mundaka, Spain, 2005

English surf rat. Me in Oceanside, California on my first ever visit to the U.S.A. 2007

Five years later in 2012 on patrol in the California desert, a million miles from the ocean and a million miles from my true self

Phil and I reunited in California. 2016

Steph and I in Nosara, Costa Rica, 2018

Surfing Trestles, San Clemente, California ,2018

Jason and I somewhere in Baja, Mexico, 2018

CORE SURFING

What is core surfing? I am not talking about fitness. I am talking about you, me, and every surfer—the blue-collar surfers who fit in a session where they can, before or after work, or as weekend warriors; the ones who ride duct taped boards and wear patched up wetsuits; the guy who surfs under the California marine layer after grabbing morning coffee and battling traffic for an hour only to find that all the good parking spots are taken, the meter is broken, and there are already fifty surfers out; the girl in Cornwall who woke up before sunrise and drove to a freezing beach only to find onshore winds and two-foot waves, but she paddled out anyways in a five-millimeter wetsuit, hood, boots, and gloves. *We* are surfing's   core.

Realizing you are surfing's core can be empowering. Once you are hooked on surfing and in the club, you can become a member of any of the numerous subcultures of surfing. Perhaps longboarding gets your juices flowing—the style and grace of long, drawn out turns and walking the board. Maybe you want to be the next John John Florence? Chances are, if you are younger you will be influenced by someone from the mainstream. By all means, do explore, but remember that the lifestyle will come in time. Surfing is a sport, and once you indulge and practice enough it becomes a lifestyle. Surfing becomes part of us, and as it flourishes in our consciousness it organically points us in directions. Spending that much time so close to nature will undoubtedly make you an environmentalist of some sort. Travel will come also. Your curiosity and interest in far-off lands and elusive, perfect waves will steep and mature inside of you. Surfing will teach you lessons both in and out of water.

When I was a lanky, awkward seventeen-year-old lad, I was all about the punk rock surf scene. I wore Lost t-shirts and baggy board shorts and rode shortboards. Well, I tried to ride shortboards. With the clarity of hindsight, I realize I stepped onto a shortboard about one year too early and probably halted my progress substantially. I see it time and time again with new surfers. After standing up in the whitewater one hundred times, one wants to get to the next step. Most wrongly decide the next step is buying and riding a shorter board like the surfers on posters or in videos. Buying a shortboard too soon will absolutely stunt your progress. Larger boards equal more waves, more waves equal more practice, more practice equals progression, and progression equals more fun!

To be fair, when I was two years into my surfing life, I cared equally about progress *and* looking cool. At least in my mind the shortboard made me look cool on the beach, but in the water I looked like the beginner I was. I struggled to catch waves and could barely control the board, if and when I did stand up.

Surfing can make one very self-conscious, especially as a teenager. I used to be unreasonably aware of people noticing me on and off the beach. We all need a good humbling moment every now and then to realize that no one *really* cares all that much, whether in the form of a wipeout or something else.

For me it was something else. When I was about nineteen, I was humbled like never before. My friend, Nick, and I were walking down to the water's edge on a rare eighty-degree summer day at Fistral Beach in Newquay, England. Fistral is the most famous surfing beach in England and gets rammed with tourists in the summer. The beach was packed that day with girls to try to show off to, and the waves were firing—a perfect four-foot ramp with offshore winds and groomed lines. At this point, Nick and I could hold our own in the water and put some decent enough looking turns together. So, like most teenage boys, we were eager to impress some of the girls on the beach. We were bound to stand out, especially since there were what seemed like six million beginner surfers knocking around the shore. *Sure, we'll give you a lesson, ladies.*

With our shortboards under our arms we meandered down the hot sand, dodging the grockles and inlanders. We spotted a group of girls about our age that were tanning near the shore. Nick and I looked at each other and instantly knew where we were going to paddle out. We pulled up at the water's edge a few yards in front of the girls and began strapping our leashes on. This was the first time Nick had not paddled off without me. One of the girls called out to in a curious northern accent and asked if we were going out into the giant waves. I quickly replied, "Yeah, wanna come?" With a smile the girl replied, "Nah, we'll just watch." Nick and I laughed as we thought luck was on our side. With confidence oozing from my nineteen-year-old spirit, I began to walk out into the water alongside Nick. I was confident in four-foot surf and knew that easy takeoffs and smooth sections awaited us. What could go wrong?

As the water level reached our knees, I noticed a wave coming right for us. In our eagerness to impress, it seemed we hadn't bothered to notice the shorebreak. We hadn't watched the sets or the inside waves. We had been too concerned about looking cool and showing off. What we were now noticing, as we stood ten yards in the ocean with our boards under our arms and the girls watching, was that the waves were really jacking up on the inside, and there was quite an aggressive and frightening shorebreak wave approaching us. It seemed the waves were perfect on the outside, but as they died out in deeper water, they continued to travel and reform on the inside into heavy, thick beasts that were demolishing tourists into the sand with malice and intent. We were stranded in no man's land. We were too far down the beach to go back and not far enough to make a quick paddle out beyond the danger. We were about to get smashed like the pair of muppets we were.

At that point, we both attempted a different strategy to save ourselves and gambled with odds against us. I decided to turn and run. Nick attempted to duck dive; it didn't work. I watched him as the wave reared its ugly head above us, about to slap us both with the lip. Nick pushed his board down into the water to try and sink it and dive under the wave. The only problem was that all the water had just been sucked up the face of the wave. Nick was pushing his board into sand only, and all the water was above him and about to crash down. He was crouching like a frog and didn't look so cool anymore. At the same time, I turned and took two steps up the beach before I looked over my shoulder and witnessed Nick get absolutely obliterated by the wave. I then awaited the inevitable and threw my board to the side.

That wave really did feel like a slap in the back of the head, and not any old slap, but a real stinging, open-palmed pummel to the chops. Down I went face-first into the sand, mere yards from the dry beach and humiliating sound of laughter coming from the ladies. I have to say, being washed up a beach, face-down and lying in my own red-faced shame next to the girls I was trying to impress, was one of the more distressing moments of my teenage years. I wobbled to my feet to see Nick had suffered the same fate. He was up and dusting himself off. We both laughed nervously at each other without looking at the girls.

Instinctively, we both headed back into the cauldron of the Atlantic Ocean. Nick was gone, paddling straight out and not looking back. There was no messing around this time. I was proud of him. *That's it, dude, we won't let that happen again. Let's redeem ourselves.* As I watched Nick make it past the shorebreak and safely away from the embarrassment, I realized I was still standing in the shorebreak, and another wave was approaching. I was about to get another beat down. Why was I still standing there? Powerlessness is the most humbling feeling in the world. I took a deep breath, shrugged my shoulders, and let Mother Nature teach me a second lesson for the day. Once again, I washed ashore at the feet of the bronzed ladies like the pathetic shrimp I was in that moment. I got up, grabbed my board, and walked one hundred yards south while staring at the floor. I then paddled out without issue and made sure I never crossed paths with those girls again.

I think that lesson in humiliation was a turning point for me. It was a catalyst to stop taking myself so seriously, to stop caring what others thought of me, and to start having more fun. Why was I riding a shortboard that wasn't even that fun? Why was I only wearing one brand of clothing? Why was I so easily influenced by the mainstream? I was constantly comparing myself to others instead of just being myself. Theodore Roosevelt once said, "Comparison is the thief of joy." I have never forgotten that quote. I have never owned a conventional shortboard since.

In this modern world nothing is sacred. If there is a buck to be made from something then someone will make it, and you can't blame anyone for doing so. Everyone's value system differs. Some value money over experience while others value family most. To each their own. As surfers, our value systems also differ. It is a lot easier now that I am older and supposedly wiser to not care what people think of me. I choose to ride the boards I want in the style I want. I would identify as a retro-style surfer. I ride twin fins, eggs, logs, and anything "fun." Does that mean I've been influenced by a different subculture? Maybe.

Maybe I'm as guilty as the next man who buys into the surf industry and helps fuel it. It's easy. I throw on my Fitzroy hoody, Rainbow sandals, and generic surf-branded t-shirt and am good to go. Personally, I admire those who don't buy into the surf brands. Those who wear whatever they want and don't need to wear a t-shirt based on a hobby that they partake in on weekends. When you look at it that way, it is ridiculous. I probably look like a thirty-three-year-old teenager.

These days the big surf brands are so far removed from the core surfer. We have recently witnessed the two biggest surf brands of all time go bust and eventually merge. Why? Probably because they gave up on the core and went after the almighty dollar. I don't blame them. In my basic understanding of business, it makes total sense. They are businesses, and the purpose of a business is to turn a profit, especially a business with shareholders.

Most big surf brands started out as core surf companies, and some were started by well-known surfers. As a company grows and becomes successful, it is often sold to a giant corporate parent company. It becomes part of a cycle for which there are pros and cons. The biggest benefit is that it presents an opportunity for the next up-and-coming core surf brand to start out in someone's garage. Maybe that company will also succeed and be purchased one day. The cycle continues.

If that is the case, why would I wear a brand that now has less to do with surfing and more to do with major fashion industry brands? Those once core surf brands moved out of surf shops and into department stores. In my opinion, if I'm going to wear a fashion brand, I may as well wear something that doesn't make me look like an adolescent beach bum.

It seems to me that there are two very distinct surf worlds: the upper industry and the core. The upper industry contains all the major surf brands and the World Surf League (WSL), which, for those who do not know, is the governing body of competitive surfing. Even some major surfboard manufacturers have deserted the average surfer and core market in search of expansion in profit. There simply isn't a large enough market in selling to just surfers.

The major brands and the WSL have a mission to make surfing go mainstream. Quicksilver wants to sell t-shirts to dads shopping in Macy's, and the WSL wants to sell to someone who lives in Kansas and has never surfed before so that they have something to throw on to watch a surf competition and go the local wave pool. That's ok, it's inevitable. It might even work. The UFC got millions of people who had no interest in fighting ten years ago to pay to watch combat sports on a Saturday night. With the advent of performance wave pools, the future looks very bright or dark for surfing, depending on which side of the divide you stand.

Either way, the core average surfers are starting to be ignored due to the elite industry becoming more and more detached from surfing. For me, they are two distinct worlds. I like to view the elite from afar by watching a competition now and again, but I am quite happy staying in my average surfer's world.

Surfboard shapers are not immune from this either. Certain surfboard big brands have monopolized the professional competitive tour. Is that down to the quality of the product? Elite professional surfers probably aren't making wrong choices in surfboards, but at the same time, you can't tell me that only three surfboard manufacturers in the world have boards worth riding. If you looked at the top thirty surfers in the competitive world and what they are riding you could be forgiven for assuming so. It seems to come down to marketing and mass production.

I have ridden a few boards from major manufacturers, and there is no denying that they are quality products and should be sold for $800 a piece. However, they are not of superior quality in comparison to some of the locally shaped boards I ride. My quiver at the moment consists of one widely known shaper and four local shapers. If a local shaper makes a quality product at half the price, it's a no-brainer for me.

Next time you're thinking of buying a new board or some new threads, think local. There are many misconceptions to buying local. Most think it will be more expensive, but quite often it may be cheaper. There are also the many benefits of local service and loyalty rewards. In other words, get to know your local brands and build a relationship with these businesses. Help them grow, and keep the cycle going. Maybe one day, when you are older and walking with your children around Macy's, you'll be able to buy that cool, local, underground brand you once sported as a kid.

LIFETIME FITNESS

I'm thirty-three, and there are some days that I feel it. However, I am surfing the best I have ever surfed in my life. I owe that in part to a guy I met at a Slightly Stoopid concert in England many years ago. I was at an after-party near Fistral Beach. I began talking to a stranger about surfing in a dimly lit bar playing loud reggae music. I think it was a hotel owned by Quicksilver. The American stranger gave me some advice that I heeded some years later. He told me that if I really loved surfing that much, I needed to move closer to good surf. The guy was from California, and he was right. Just like the man with the tattooed face in Oceanside, I owe this man a beer.

At the time I met the prophet from California, I lived in a location that did have surfable waves, but good surf was far from consistent. Now I live in California and surf as much as I can. As simple as it sounds, surfing more is the first key to progression in any serious surfing life. The more you surf, the better you'll be. It's obvious. Living near consistent surf helps a lot.

Fitness is also a key factor. Fitness is something I overlooked most of my surfing life. In my younger years it didn't matter. I ate what I wanted and stayed thin and lean. I could surf for six hours and not think twice about it. Things are much different now. Injuries are easier to sustain, and use of the gym, swimming pool, and heavy bag now play an essential role in my surfing life.

I was roughly twenty-five when I started putting on weight. I was in the midst of a dark period of my life, and the weight seemed to creep up on me after being lean my entire life. At the time, I surfed less and less and lived two hours from the beach. Before I knew it, I hadn't surfed for months at a time. I was concentrating on other things in my life, such as my career, and I wasn't paying attention to myself—my true self. I had lost any kind of spiritual and healthy balance to my life.

At one point, I went from 190 pounds to almost 235 pounds, and losing focus of myself and frankly having no interest in diet or health was to blame. I had never needed to have an interest in diet. I had always been as skinny as a rake and ate what I liked. Now I was paying the price for being ignorant and out of touch with my true being. Like any bad habit, poor dietary habits and poor fitness routines are hard to change. Like an addiction, my brain liked the false rewards from eating junk food. Changing these cycles and behaviors is very difficult, but it can be done if and only when one truly wants to change.

I would still surf every now and then during that period of poor health. I was awful. The extra weight and bad health choices, limited my time in the water to an hour or so, and I couldn't get waves. To give myself a paddling advantage I rode boards I didn't want to ride, and I didn't enjoy my surfing at all. But change did come, like it always does. Change comes when one is truly ready and willing or when one is forced by circumstance. Sometimes we must make hard decisions and face tough challenges in order to change.

There are so many diets and fitness programs out there that may or may not work for you. Most did not work for me. For me, change must be honest and sustainable. It needs to be something I can stick to, not just three weeks from now but three years from now. For example, it's all well and good saying you are going to be a vegan or to try the latest fad diet, but you need to determine if your circumstances and surroundings will support your changes to make them sustainable. If you eat red meat every day and enjoy it, it's probably going to be tough to become a vegan. Add to that your circumstances or surroundings. Where do you work? What is your daily routine and commute? What is your lunch routine? It's not going to be very sustainable for you to be a vegan if you work in a BBQ restaurant or if you go to lunch at a steakhouse every Friday with that person you are trying to impress from the office. You would need the willpower of a saint. That's a drastic example, but your circumstances must meet your expectations in order to make real sustainable changes. It makes things a lot easier if you are realistic and honest with yourself.

When I was in my teens, I smoked a lot of marijuana—a lot. I got high every day from the age of fifteen to the age of twenty. It was my lifestyle, and it fit in with my surroundings. My circumstances were perfect for it. I was a teenage boy living for waves, and all my friends smoked. I was happy in that lifestyle, and I didn't want to change a thing. By the time I was twenty or so, I was done. I no longer enjoyed smoking. I got bored of the lifestyle and wanted to change, but my circumstances made it difficult. I was still in the same place in life and surrounded by the same people. For some, willpower may be enough; for me it wasn't. Finally, I moved to the U.S. and never smoked habitually again. My surroundings changed, and I was able to make sustainable changes I could live by.

The same example can be used for my eating habits and fitness routine. It wasn't until I became single and motivated to lead a new life that I started taking my health more seriously. I did try some diets and other theories, none of which worked at first because they weren't sustainable. I was still eating too much fast food. That stopped when my job changed, and I had a new commute and work schedule. Once my circumstances and surroundings changed I felt free to make better choices. I chose to go to the gym more often. At first, I tried to go to the gym in the mornings, but it wasn't happening. I had to be honest with myself—I am not the best morning person. I would love to be one of those guys who wakes up at 5 a.m., reads the paper, walks the dog, and is in the lineup to surf by sunrise. I just can't do it. Even with surfing, which I love, I struggle to get up on time for dawn raids, often leaving my frustrated friends waiting at my door in the dark. I had to be honest, and the solution was simple. I would go to the gym at night, every night. I seemed to have more energy at night, and I was lucky enough to have a job that finished at a decent time so that I could get to the gym and run a few miles on the treadmill each evening. This was sustainable for me. The other thing I learned regarding fitness was to be honest and keep it simple. It is very easy to get lost down a rabbit hole of diets, fads, theories, and fitness classes. What I try to remember is that basic weight gain and loss comes down to science. In general, we need to burn more calories than we take in. Obviously, it is more complex than that as other things come into play, such as how many calories are burned daily at rest, diet, and metabolism. But if you eat relatively healthy and exercise enough each day to burn an extra five hundred calories, you'll end up losing weight. It won't happen all that quickly, and the number on the scale will fluctuate from day to day. With that, I suggest only taking into account the weight displayed every other Friday morning. If you only log that weight biweekly rather than check your weight daily, you will likely see a steady decline.

I designed my fitness plan around surfing. I wanted to be stronger, leaner, faster, and more flexible. At first, I tried to do it the easy way, thinking more surfing alone would do it. After all, what better way to get in shape for surfing *than* surfing. However, for me, surfing wasn't enough. I had to add extra activities. My main weight loss tool was and still is the treadmill or an outdoor run. I find that four miles burns around 500 calories in one go. If I run too much I do get some pain in my knees, so I switch it up with swimming laps in a pool. This benefits me the same way with burning calories, although I may not burn quite as many calories as I would running. It also helps build and tone muscle. I also practice breath holds and underwater swimming to prepare me for wipeouts. Alongside these main activities, I work in resistance training to build muscle and strength. Find what works for you and make it sustainable. The more activities you enjoy the better, that way you can mix it up.

I have been lucky so far in life. I haven't suffered any major injuries. Recently, I witnessed my good friend, Garrett, suffer a very serious ankle injury that will take him out of the water for at least a year. I can't imagine what I would do in that situation. The worst surfing injuries I have suffered were from my fins, boards, and stingrays. The most *painful* injury I suffered was from a stingray.

At the time of writing this I have been stung five times by stingrays—once in San Clemente and the other four in Huntington Beach. If you have surfed Huntington Beach in the summer, you are probably aware of the infestation of stingrays, especially the further north you go towards Bolsa Chica State Beach. For me, the worst thing about a sting is the fairly manageable pain and the fact that the next four hours of your life will be wasted with your foot in a bucket of extremely hot water. After the hot water has broken down the proteins in the poison then you are normally good to go. That's what happened to me the first four times I was stung, but the fifth time was different.

It was a sunny, warm January day at Ninth Street in Huntington Beach, and the surf was small but fun. I was surfing with my friend, Jason, and we were just finishing up our session. Jason was already on the beach waiting while I was searching for *one more wave*. I was always taught never to say, "one more wave." I was told if you say that then something bad will happen. It could be something minor like having no waves show up, and then you'll sit there like a lemon for an hour. Or it could be something worse, like getting stung by a stingray.

Huntington Beach is a frustrating wave sometimes, as it was on this particular day. The tide was wrong for the conditions, resulting in quite a common setup for Huntington Beach—the setup where the wave breaks outside for twenty yards and then dies out to a non-existent swell line through the deeper water known as the Chuck hole. This is where the famous Huntington Hop comes into play. I've become quite an expert at pumping my board through the Chuck hole. This is so you can stay on the wave and make the most of the inside section where it reforms and smashes onto the sand. It can be a fun inside section worth a hit or two or a closeout tube ride that will make you eat sand.

As Jason watched, I tried to catch the reform wave to the inside so that I can get at least one decent ride that session. I had not surfed well at all that day. I went for a small one and missed. I jumped off my board in frustration and sunk feet-first towards the sandbar. That's when I felt the old familiar sting, like a nail piercing your foot. You first feel the fin of the ray squirm. If you have ever trodden on a fish while walking out in the ocean, it feels exactly like that—a slimy squirm as the fish swims away. You feel that squirm, only with a ray, the squirm is followed by a sharp, stabbing pain as the barb strikes and enters your foot. If you've been stung before you know exactly what I'm describing. After the barb hit me, I cussed to myself, more out of annoyance and knowing the inconvenience this was going to cause the rest of the day.

I walked out and showed Jason the pea-sized wound on the sole of my foot. A little blood oozed out, and I decided to walk home. It was off season, and I didn't want to bother waiting for the one lifeguard truck tasked with patrolling the whole beach at that time of year. I lived a two-minute walk up the street anyway.

I hobbled back to my place and placed my foot in the bathtub. Jason made sure I was ok and headed home. It was no big deal, just a routine stingray strike, and the pain wasn't as bad as previous stings I had experienced. I bathed for an hour or two, hobbled around the house the rest of the day, and went to bed that night hoping the swell would come up a foot or two the next day for a better session.

The next morning it didn't matter what the waves were doing, as judging by the state of my foot, I wouldn't be surfing them. I woke up to my ankle and foot swollen the size of a grapefruit. I iced my ankle and foot and decided to wait another day for the swelling to go down. I didn't make it through the night. The pain incredibly worsened, and a red rash began to spread across my foot and up my ankle. I kept my ankle elevated, and anytime I let it hang down lower than my knee I'd experience excruciating pain. I went to the emergency room where I was informed that if I had waited much longer the staph infection would have spread to my blood, and I would have been in real trouble. The injury took five days to clear with a mix of antibiotics and pain medications. I developed a slight fear of stingrays ever since that fifth sting.

Surfing is inherently dangerous, and injuries can occur, especially in crowded lineups. A few summers ago, I was hit at full speed in the hip by a beginner surfer on a pointed fiberglass shortboard. It caused a lot of pain and bruising. The surfer's response to me was, "Sorry, man, sometimes it's just too much fun to turn!" What he meant to say is, "Sorry, man, I am not a competent surfer yet, and I am riding a board that I can't control." I guess it's all good, we've all been there. My friend, Boris, can attest to that.

When I was a few months into my surfing life, I was surfing at Saunton while riding Boris' own board, the yellowed Superfrog. I was riding the old battered beast and caught a whitewater wave. I scrambled to my feet and headed to the shore at full speed with a wide-eyed grin. A similar wide-eyed grin was the last thing I saw on Boris' face before I smashed into him. I still can't figure out to this day why he was smiling as an 8-foot fiberglass missile was heading straight towards him. The board hit him square in the chin with a loud crack that wiped the grin off his face. I felt terrible, and the incident ended both of our sessions. Somehow, nothing was broken, and all his teeth were intact. Injuries can happen in surfing, and time out of the water is a negative experience for any surfer, both physically and mentally. But injuries happen in all sports, and having the right approach towards surfing can only help the situation.

Changing your approach to surfing is important. Seeing it like any other sport is critical. Most sports you must train for and be in shape. Surfing should be no different. Surfing comes with all kinds of stigmas attached to it, the lazy beach bum stereotype being the most outdated. Surfers are some of the most fit and healthy athletes out there. We are lucky we get a full body workout while doing what we love the most. After all, the best workout is the one where you don't even know you're working out.

TRAVEL

My first real international surf trip was in 2005. I was twenty years old and had never left England, other than for couple of day trips to France with my high school. Boris, Phil, and I decided to go to Mundaka, Spain. Why? I have no idea. I also have no idea what we thought we were going to do once we got to there. Mundaka is a notoriously fickle left-hand point break in the Basque region of northern Spain. It is a wave of elite level caliber and was a stop on the world tour for surfing professionals for many years. It doesn't break all that often, but when it does it offers incredibly heavy barrels and long rides. At least that's what I have read. I wouldn't know because Mundaka was flat as a pancake for the fourteen days we were there.

My skill level at the time gave me no business whatsoever in the lineup at Mundaka. I sometimes wonder if we would have been naive enough to paddle out had the wave broken while we were there.

We were naive and stupid enough to smuggle some marijuana in our board bags and leashes across international borders on that trip, but that's another story. We still had an amazing time.

The Basque region of northern Spain is unique and beautiful. It has a strong cultural history and fights a fierce case for independence from Spain and France. This independence movement led to low tourism numbers in the 1980s and 90s due a terrorist bombing campaign by separatist group ETA. I remember seeing the "wanted" posters all over town and on bus stops. Still today, northern Spain is not as heavily populated with tourists as southern Spain or the Costa del Sol. Plus, it has some great surf, it just didn't when we were there.

On that trip, because of the conditions, we ended up surfing in other areas along the northern coast, such as Bakio and San Sebastián. The surf was terrible, about knee-high and onshore, for two weeks. It didn't matter to us, though. We were on an adventure and wanted to surf anything that was offered.

Boris, Phil, and I had grown up and surfed together since day one. Boris was the kind of guy you wanted at a party or on a surf trip. He was unpredictable and always made us laugh by cracking jokes to the limits of decency. He was also a keen drinker of Scrumpy Jack cider or anything alcoholic for that matter. For those not familiar with west country cider, it is the drink of choice for most in the four western-most counties of England. Locals have been producing their own pressed and fermented apples for hundreds of years. We would often stop at a local farm and buy some locally made "jug 'o' shite" on route to a surfing weekend. Sometimes it was so bright yellow it was almost luminous. As for the pulp, that stuff could be lethal; maybe not lethal but definitely liver-damaging and somewhat hallucinogenic, on occasion. Good stuff. Recently, I have seen a growth in the alcoholic cider market in the U.S. No offense, America, but what you are drinking is not cider, it is mildly alcoholic apple juice.

The other surfer on that trip was Phil. Phil was the opposite of Boris. Phil was tall and skinny, he had a constant smile on his face, and he was always mellow and calm. He was not as much into alcohol as Boris but enjoyed the wacky tobacky a lot, as we all did in our youth. Phil complimented any surf trip and was always willing to paddle out and surf. His enthusiasm to shred was infectious. I still surf with Phil to this day, when we get a chance to meet up somewhere in the world.

Alongside our other friend, Nick, we would go on surf trips every weekend to Cornwall or Devon. We would jump in my dark blue, 1988 Leyland Daf van, complete with a tape cassette player, board racks, and three makeshift beds. The unlucky fourth crew member would sleep in the cab across three seats. We would drive three hours west and spend two nights living rough and surfing anything we found. Sunday night we would drive back to Dorset, dreary-eyed, salty, and completely knackered. It was a great time with little responsibility and not a care in the world. We all thought those times would last forever. Little did we realize how life can change gears in an instant.

Growing up where we did in South West England in the 90s and early 2000s was somewhat routine. It was a very innocent upbringing and somewhat idealistic. Fishing, trekking through green fields, and playing in the woods were all pastimes for us rural kids on the south coast. As we all reached adolescence it became more difficult, or rather boring. We all came from middle class families. Some of us struggled more than others, but we got by. Being born in 1985 meant we were the last generation before technology really took over. It also meant our paths were somewhat mapped out for us. We all left school at sixteen and got jobs. Monday through Friday, I worked in a factory that made parts for tanks and the ministry of defense. I would sit there for nine hours a day deburring metal and looking at surf magazines. All I cared about was being able to make some money each week to buy petrol and go on weekend surf trips. As long as I had money for food, boards, and the latest surf DVD, I was good. Phil was a chef, and Boris worked in the same factory as I. Later in our early twenties we all made decisions to move on in our lives, but our late teenage years were all about adventure and surfing.

The trip to Mundaka was our first real surf trip. As usual, we had no idea what we were doing. We bought plane tickets and packed a tent, surfboards, and our travel rucksacks. That was it. Off we went. We arrived in the airport in Bilbao and collected our boards from the terminal. We headed outside and hailed a cab. It didn't stop, and neither did the next one or the one after that. Eventually, an old Spanish cab driver stopped to tell us we needed to call for a cab that could accommodate the boards. *That makes sense.*

None of us could speak Spanish, but somehow we managed to summon a cab big enough for Boris' 6'10 magic carpet, my 6'0 round nose fish, and Phil's 5'10 fish. The driver couldn't speak English, but as we would notice on numerous occasions on that trip, annoyance and irritation translates just fine without words; we understood the driver loud and clear on that one. Boris was in the front seat, and Phil and I were in the back. The cab driver asked, "Adónde quieres ir?" Me and Phil looked at each other and laughed like school boys. Boris did his best to engage the driver, and as if he was speaking to a five-year-old alien replied, "Mooon-daaa-ka!" The driver clearly had no idea what or where Mundaka was. He also looked half terrified and half amused at the bearded white man yelling at him. After five or so minutes of Boris trying to speak a language he had never learned, Phil pulled out a map. He handed it to Boris who pointed at the outcrop on the north coast. Finally, the driver caught on, "Aaaaaah, Mundaka, sí." The driver smiled, and off we went.

Having no accommodation or plans to speak of, we somehow managed to get through that fourteen-day period quite successfully. We stayed on a camp site in town, got drunk every night, surfed crappy waves everyday, rode busses to beaches we had never heard of, and ate amazing food. Surf travel is about adventure, the unknown, and the search for waves and undiscovered spots. That trip ignited a passion for surf travel in us, and the three of us travelled well and wide in the years that followed. Phil has been barreled in Indo, Boris has gotten drunk and walked through paper walls in China, and I ended up living in California. We all still travel today and don't have plans on stopping anytime soon. One has to keep travel a priority in life; it is a secondary form of education, and we should never stop learning new things about our wonderful world.

Travel is an essential part of being a surfer, average or not. Once you feel you are at a certain level as a surfer that is no longer beginner, you start to build a lifestyle around surfing. Traveling becomes a huge part of that lifestyle.

So why do so many get stuck in the trap of day-to-day adult life? Why do we stop traveling? Some people even stop surfing regularly, maybe fitting in a session once every few months. For me, that is unacceptable. As an average surfer, where do we fit into the surfing world as it relates to traveling? There are certainly waves that are beyond my skill level, and I have no plans on paddling out at those places until I progress further. But, there is an absolute bounty of beautiful places around the world with amazing waves and cultures to explore.

Over the next few chapters, I have compiled a guide of sorts to some of the places I have been in the last few years. These were places I found to be perfect for average surfers to progress and feel comfortable.

ENGLAND

England may not be the first place you think of when you think of surf destinations. Nevertheless, that is where I chose to begin my average surfer journey. It's familiar. I spent twenty-two years of my life there, and I have an attachment to the rugged beauty and open spaces of the West Country.

The contrast from Orange County to the U.K. is striking. California is bright, not just in climate and weather but in consumption and advertising. England is dull. There are no billboards or strip malls outside of the cities, just green fields and woodland dissected by motorways. Once you start heading southbound on the motorway towards Southampton and onto the West Country, it becomes even more dull and baron yet extremely beautiful.

If you look at a map of the U.K., the West Country is the local name for the four counties that make up the peninsular sticking out in the bottom left corner:

Somerset, Dorset, Devon, and Cornwall. For the sake of surfing, you can ignore Somerset.

Dorset is the eastern most county of the three, and its only coastal exposure is the English Channel. It's more famous for fishing and its naval ports in World War II than it is for surfing. However, with a big enough swell, the energy will run up the channel and hit the many slate reefs along the south coast all the way through Dorset. Local knowledge is key to surfing this part of the region, so make friends.

I arrived at a small village in Dorset on the south coast. My arrival happened to coincide with the swell of the year. A deep southwest low-pressure system in the Bay of Biscay was promising sizeable surf for most of Western Europe. At least that's what I was told. When it comes to conditions in England, you are usually looking at close range storm surf. The problem with that is the wind will often force you to search for a sheltered cove. However, the swell that met me upon arrival was a longer-range ground swell.

The second morning after my arrival, while nursing a hangover from too many Scrumpy ciders in the pub, I met up with some old friends and headed to a reef break near a sixteenth century village. This place was a secret spot when I was growing up in England, but everyone knows about it now. We got there to find all three reefs firing with overhead faces, but howling winds were ready to ruin the party. Nonetheless, the adventure started, and the excitement was there. After all, you do have to work for your waves in England.

The next day we decided to head to Cornwall. Cornwall is the first or last county in England, depending on how you look at the map. It is one of the most beautiful places on Earth with wild open moorlands, ancient woodlands, and rocky cliffs that meet sandy beaches that stretch for miles. We were headed to a town called Newquay, the surf capital of the U.K. Unlike Dorset, where everything is more fickle and underground, Cornwall is surfing loud and proud. It is exposed to both the Atlantic Ocean and the English Channel and will pick up most swells. Newquay is the hub of the U.K. surf scene. Just like Huntington Beach or any other surf town, Newquay is filled with board rental shops and surf shops, but you'll see coats and clouds instead of bikinis and sunshine. You may have to sacrifice waves for sunshine if you visit in the summer, and even then you are not guaranteed sunshine.

On the day we arrived in Cornwall, the surf was big, and the winds had dropped. We went and checked a few spots, and the famous Fistral Beach was topping out with double overhead sets. The paddle out looked miserable. We headed through the town to Towan Beach, which looked much better at about head-high and clean.

Five-millimeter suits, gloves, boots, and hoods are all needed in England in March. We walked down to a beautiful beach with cliffs on one side and a harbor wall on the other. The waves looked a lot bigger when we stepped into the water. Then again, waves always look bigger when the sky is gray and the water is cold. I paddled out with Phil who was just back from Indo and surfing with the confidence and tan of such a man. He effortlessly paddled off and was outside in a few minutes. I, on the other hand, felt the first flush of freezing cold water go down the back of my suit and got an ice cream headache. This is England. I had been surfing California's Pacific waves for the past ten years at this point, so I figured this would be a cake-walk. I was wrong. I got beaten and battered, and it took me forever to paddle out the back. The waves were a lot bigger and more powerful than I remembered, and the current was fairly strong.

The first wave I dropped was probably about head-high. I popped up and dropped down the face into a closeout tube. It went dark and cold as I spun in the Atlantic's washing machine. I came up, and there was my board, well, technically, Phil's board. It was in two pieces. *Damn! Session over. Sorry, Phil.*

One of my favorite things about surfing cold water in England is the post-surf ritual: dry off, change into warm clothes, and head to the pub. You can't feel your hands or feet, but it feels great. A misconception of England is that the food is bad, but it's not. People that once occupied a third of the world are bound to have brought back some good recipes, so go ahead and explore the menus instead of ordering the usual fish and chips.

The next day we went to Devon, the middle county of the three, and found some fun waves. It's a little more built up than Cornwall but with waves on both coasts. It's also more of an established surf destination than Dorset but not quite as much as

Cornwall. North Devon holds some great beaches, and we got peaks to ourselves up and down the coastline. We surfed three-foot waves for the next few days before it went flat. It was uncrowded, fun, and rewarding.

Overall, the English surf scene is unique. Although there is a booming industry of shapers, clothing, and wetsuit manufacturers, and it is crowded during the summer with giant surf contests, England has somehow managed to keep an "underground" feel to its surf scene. The waves are not epic, and there are many flat spells, but the culture revolves around stories of that perfect day a few years back and the hope that the next big swell is coming. Locals are drinking in pubs and speculating the forecast and which cove or beach might light up tomorrow. It's a refreshing break from Starbucks, parking meters, and traffic. The vibe in the water is mellow, but as with anywhere, respect for locals is key. If you're looking for a different type of surfing adventure, book a flight, rent a car, pack some warm clothes, and spend a few nights in a bed and breakfast in the West Country.

MEXICO

"I'll put up a GoFundMe to pay the kidnap ransom." That was the jokingly response I received from my boss when I told him I was going to Baja, Mexico for Easter weekend. This was the typical response I collected when I told someone I was driving a few hours south of the border to go for a surf. I understand why my friends and colleagues might have responded that way, and I am sure their warnings for me not to go were born from a genuine concern for my safety. Like them, I also read the news and saw the videos. I remember the stories about the cartels, burnt-out vans, bodies hanging from bridges, car jackings, and murders, but I also long for some adventure in my life. I tend to get bored of driving to Pacific Coast Highway, paying the meter, and paddling out with fifty other guys and girls before work. Maybe I'm just spoiled.

I try to have a balanced view of media and news. I'm also an obsessive researcher. When I get an idea, I will research everything I can and plan accordingly. So, that's exactly what I did for my trip to Baja. I dove twenty Google pages deep into every article I could find about surfing, camping, traveling, and crime on the Baja peninsula. I did so with a careful eye on who the sources of the stories were and what the angle was. For instance, one set of Baja crime statistics published by a tourism board would predictably present a dramatic drop in crime for 2017, while a newspaper based on the "if it bleeds, it leads" philosophy would publish sensationalist headlines about cartel wars and the bloodiest year on record. I tried to find the middle ground as I always do with all news.

There is no doubt that Mexico is a dangerous place, one would be naive to think otherwise, but so is downtown Los Angeles. My chance of being robbed, carjacked, or even murdered in either place is much higher if I am involved in gangs or drugs; that was the general conclusion I drew after my research. I concluded that to be a victim of violent crime in Baja you must be involved in the drug trade, lacking some common sense, or just very unlucky. Hopefully, I was neither of the last two. In the end, the biggest risk to surfers seemed to be car break-ins or robbery, and I deemed the risk to reward ratio in my favor and asked my friend Jason if he wanted to join me. He said yes without hesitation. It's always great to have a buddy who is up for an adventure.

I had little to no experience in Baja other than a quick day trip over the border ten years prior. I planned accordingly. I got my truck serviced, checked the spare tires, purchased Mexican insurance, studied the maps, charts, and swells, and set my alarm for 3.30 a.m.

The next morning, Jason and I were on the road from Orange County at 4 a.m. and at the border by 5.30 a.m. We were both a little nervous as we purchased some coffee from a café that sat no more than five hundred yards from the infamous border fence. U.S. customs and border patrol agents dressed in blue police-like uniforms were crossing the street back and forth to either start or finish their shift. Jason and I were busy stashing small amounts of cash in hiding spots within my white Toyota Tacoma. The idea behind that was derived from internet advice; if we did get robbed or if my truck got broken into, the thief would only take *some* of our cash. I had fifty bucks in my wallet and scattered another eighty dollars around the truck's nooks and crannies. One cannot afford to be naive in Mexico.

It was still dark when we crossed the border. I felt butterflies in my stomach as we first drove past the Mexican border guard and then a couple of Mexican military personnel with machine guns. Neither of the guards acknowledged us as we smiled at them and drove off into the unknown.

We crossed the border and kept to the right lane that lead towards the coast and would take us along the northern edge of Tijuana. According to some online sources, Tijuana is a city with the highest crime rate in Baja. Since murders and kidnappings seemed somewhat common in this area, we didn't want to take a wrong turn, even if my research suggested we'd be fine.

You immediately know you're in a different country when you cross the border. I don't think there are many borders in the world that you can cross by land that have such contrasting worlds and cultures. Mexico is an underdeveloped country with real poverty and hardship. It is also a country of pride, passion, and wonderful people who are welcoming, respectful, and friendly. As the sun rose over the hills and mountains in my rear-view mirror, we could see the giant, foreboding border wall on our right and the run-down, shantytown-like slums of Tijuana on our left. It was incredible to think this place was only about two to three hours from the manicured lawns of suburban Orange County. It's a different world entirely.

We continued towards the coast and hugged the toll road to the west and then south towards our destination. With every mile that passed under my truck's tires we felt more relaxed as our nerves dissipated. We were chatting and laughing while doing our best to read and translate the Spanish signposts and road signs. We barely saw another car the whole way and began to feel a little ridiculous about having been worried or apprehensive about the trip. It was too easy.

We passed numerous surf breaks we had read about and chose to ignore. We were headed about 60 miles south of the border. The swell had been small and extremely poor most of the week on the entire west coast. It wasn't any better that day, but we had a plan. According to the forecast patterns, the swell and wind directions were optimal for one beach in particular. Even though the swell was tiny, our destination was supposed to be a swell magnifier, meaning we could add an extra foot or two to the forecast. That was the hope, anyway. As we continued south and passed the beachfront homes and unfinished coastal developments, we witnessed that most breaks were flat or in the one-foot region. It was not looking good. We figured we would end up eating fish tacos and leaving our boards in the truck.

We paid a couple of two-dollar tolls and made it to our destination by 6.45 a.m. As I pulled off the old coast highway and onto the dirt track, I saw the first good waves rolling towards the coast. The gamble had paid off. Pretty solid combo lines were on the horizon, and the wind was almost non-existent and offshore. We began to hoot and holler at each other. How often does a gamble like that pay off? We even had the perfect boards with us to maximize the fun. A couple of twin keel fin fishes sat in the truck bed, ready and primed for the adventure. As we rambled through the exit of a dirt lot towards the cliff's edge we were greeted by incredible looking waves, stray dogs, and a few local families waking up from their tented slumbers and cooking breakfast on grills. I could not wait to paddle out.

For a couple of surfers from Southern California, the next thought I had was hard to comprehend. *Where were the surfers*?? I saw some of the best waves I had seen in months crashing along the coastline and multiple dolphins splashing around, but I didn't see any surfers. Not one. I didn't even see any surfboards in the parking lot. It was inconceivable to us, but it didn't matter; we were stoked.

The only thing that wasn't perfect at that point was the weather. It was chilly, and a thick fog and marine layer hung over the beach, although that wasn't going to ruin anything for us. We suited up and headed down a steep, neglected trail, following a rusty handrail towards the beach. As I was thinking to myself that I wouldn't want to cut my hand on the rusty handrail, I smashed my little toe against a rock. My toenail came off, and my toe busted open. *Damn.* It hurt pretty bad, and now I had a decision to make. I performed a quick inspection of my toe and deemed it not significant enough to ruin the trip, so we took our first steps onto the sand and into Baja's Pacific Ocean. The water was freezing!

We paddled out over some amazing, fun, and clean looking waves charging towards the beach. It was high tide, and the wave was breaking on the far outside with a crumbling, sloping, and inviting shoulder. As it approached the beach, it would slow down a little and then stand up on the inside for a fast mini tube or a few steep sections. It had been a bad winter for waves in California, and I hadn't seen a wave that clean and well-formed for months. I was so happy and excited that I was literally yelling.

We got to the outside and gave each other a fist bump. I no longer felt the pain in my toe, probably due to the cold water and adrenaline. The first set approached—a four-footer lined up for Jason. He paddled, and I gave him a cheer. As he took off heading south on the face of a perfect right-hander, I watched as he cruised at speed up and down, effortlessly being pushed with no cutbacks needed, three turns, then four, top to bottom, and into the shallows. The wave expired, and I heard Jason yell out in delight. He paddled back towards me with a smile and threw a shaka in my direction.

I still couldn't believe there were no other surfers out. I am usually pretty quiet and keep to myself in a lineup, but here I was a little louder and had no insecurities about showing my excitement. Neither did Jason. I could also pick any wave I wanted with no competition, and I wanted one bad.

I had a GoPro stashed in my chest zip to capture our day and make a video journal. I decided to keep it in my suit for the first few waves. I sometimes refer to the GoPro as "the curse" because when I pull it out I tend to surf badly and miss waves. I wanted to enjoy these waves, so the camera stayed stashed for the first few.

My first wave came a minute or two after Jason rejoined me out back. It was a long, left-hander all the way to the beach. It was so clean that it was easy to surf. I got a couple of top to bottom turns, a cutback, and a small head dip on the inside. As far as I was concerned, the trip was now worth it.

The session continued for three full hours of uninterrupted surfing. Two others guys did eventually paddle out, but they were small specks in the far distance on the south end of the beach. The sun came out, but the water was cold, just not cold enough to end the session early.

When our session did end, we walked back up the trail to find my truck with all windows and locks intact. The dirt lot was filling up with local families and their grills as they began celebrating Easter weekend. Everyone was friendly and smiling, and the vibe was relaxed. As morning turned to afternoon we saw a few more California license plates pulling up and a few surfers paddling out.

We ate lunch and each had a beer in a little restaurant overlooking the bluff and debated on a second session. The wind was rising and bumping up the waves a little, so we decided against it. We decided to hike around the bluff, take in the views, and daydream of all the empty surf spots around the next cove. We chatted about what it would be like on a ninety-degree summer day, just us and the waves.

We headed back north towards the U.S., and after the inevitably long wait in line to get into San Diego, we rejoined the hustle and bustle of Southern California. Our souls were satisfied for the day, and we were already dreaming of the next adventure.

A part of me didn't want to write this chapter. After all, why would I want to advertise this to others? The beauty of that trip was the uncrowded surf. On the other hand, I fear for the businesses and the surf spots in Baja. If the local economy is not getting tourist dollars from surfers, they will look elsewhere. It has already started with developments of harbors and docks for yachts. There is a plan to turn the west coast of Baja into a seafaring destination for rich tourists. It has already started, and we have already lost two surf spots due to development. Surfers should visit Baja to spend some cash and enjoy the waves.

If you are happy with crowded lineups, traffic, and closed-out waves then—by all means—stay in Southern California. If you long for adventure and uncrowded waves, then load up your truck and head south. I am already planning my next trip. The further south you head the more uncrowded it gets, and you can camp on the beach and have a true off-the-grid surf trip. All this just a few hours from Southern California. Let's go!

The other stop on my recent travels to Mexico was much further south to Sayulita. During my research I came across a few articles regarding shark activity in Mexico. I remembered my first trip to Mexico many years ago. It wasn't that far from the border. The other beaches I had passed on my way down all had surfers out. But the one I decided to stop at didn't; it was all mine, just me and a burnt-out truck on the beach.

I changed on the sand and paddled out into the green water. I spent the first half-hour figuring out the waves. It was mainly a right-hander, so I wasn't entirely comfortable as I was surfing on my back hand. Nevertheless, the waves were fun. As time passed I noticed many locals gathering on top off the bluff and staring down on the beach. First, maybe five guys, then ten, then twenty. *Surely these guys had seen better surfers than me out here?*

After about two hours my shoulders were spent, and I headed back to land. I grabbed my stuff and walked back up the dirt track towards my car. As I was walking past the men on the cliff, one of them shouted towards me.

"You're loco, amigo!"

I looked up to see a gruff Hispanic fisherman walking towards me. I laughed and smiled, not knowing for sure what he was getting at, and replied half-heartedly, "It's ok, the waves are small today."

"No, no friend," the fisherman shouted in good English, "you're crazy, man, the shark!"

"The shark?"

"Sí, a bull shark has been swimming around this beach for the last three days!"

"Well, thanks for telling me, amigo," I said with sarcasm. The fisherman laughed, and so did I, although mine was not totally sincere. The fisherman walked away, and I continued back towards my car. I couldn't believe they were watching and waiting for my imminent violent death or dismemberment. I wondered if they were taking bets. Oh well, I survived.

I have surfed with sharks, albeit unknowingly, a few times since. The first great white shark I saw up close was in Huntington Beach at 17th Street. I was surfing with just two other guys on a less than great summer evening. When surfing in Huntington Beach it is extremely common to encounter dolphins in the summer, almost at every session. Dolphins are usually sighted in groups and are easily identifiable by their light colors, curvature, and swimming patterns. It was routine to see them playing, even up close. On this day I sat out back waiting for a set wave when I noticed a fin roughly ten yards away. I immediately knew it was not a dolphin. The size, color, and swimming patterns were completely different. The fin appeared much darker with a glistening trail of water running down it. It was also twice as big and triangular, just like in movies. The magnificent creature was cruising northbound from the pier at a leisurely pace. I looked at the other surfer who sat another ten yards inside of me. We exchanged looks and words to confirm what we had just seen and paddled towards the beach. I guess I only had to paddle faster than him to stay alive.

I was strangely calm each time I saw a great white shark in the water. Each with similar circumstances. I am of the consensus that if you can see the fin and the shark is cruising by, then it already knows you are there and has no interest. Don't get me wrong, I will still head towards the beach, but I will try not to panic.

The most recent sighting I had was again in Huntington Beach. I was surfing with Steph, who spotted it first. This time it was about fifty yards outside, and judging by the splashing and ruckus, it was attacking and feeding on something, most likely a stingray. I told Steph that we were fine. I had never seen her paddle and catch a wave so fast and effortlessly in my life. She got a bomb all the way to the beach and stayed there.

After a little more research on Sayulita, I deemed the shark risk minimal and kept my shark findings from my travel buddies. The trip to Sayulita included Steph and our two other surfing friends, Jason and Sam, a married couple from Orange County. Full of positivity and longing for adventure, they are the perfect surf trip companions. Jason is a tall, skinny, trendy guy. His hair is always neatly groomed, and he likes to dress sharp, which is a challenge for most surfers. I have honestly never met such a positive human. He is always smiling, laughing, and looking for the best in people and situations. Sam is much the same but with a fierce sense of humor. When I was introduced to the group she was first to understand my dry British humor and sarcasm. That can be a problem for a Brit in the states. It can take a while for Americans to catch on. Many people think I am being serious when I am really cracking a joke. It gets a little awkward sometimes. Maybe I am just not that funny?

The competitiveness between Jason and Sam in the water is comical, and a little pronounced at times— definitely more comical, though. It's a healthy competition that probably benefits their surfing skills in the long run. I was told it used to be much, much worse with drop ins, burns, and harsh words between them. To be fair, though, there is an unspoken competitiveness between all surfers in a lineup.

I like to think of my surfing style as laid back and smooth. I prefer cruising top to bottom on retro style boards. My current quiver consists of a 9'4 log, a 7'2 mini log, a 6'0 twin fin, and numerous other "cruisers." My favorite board at this moment was my '70s-inspired twin, and knowing Sayulita had some cruisy waves, I was hopeful my average skills would suffice.

Sayulita was to be a quick five-day trip to see what it was all about. Sayulita was a place I didn't know much about other than having seen pictures of graceful longboarders cruising atop a tropical looking wave. My first surprise was the cost of the airfare. We flew in late April, but I was shocked to see the prices almost equaling a flight to Europe. We ended up booking a connecting flight to Mexico City and then a short flight to Puerto Vallarta, where we were greeted by military vehicles with mounted machine guns. Many people I spoke to prior to our trip expressed concerns regarding the current political environment in Mexico and the power struggle with cartels. Personally, I wasn't concerned. As I mentioned, you can wander into the wrong part of Los Angeles and meet your end by that same logic. At least here I could do so chasing better waves. From Puerto Vallarta, it's a short 45-minute drive to Nayarit, and you are in an incredibly beautiful part of the world surrounded by mountains and lush green forest.

The town of Sayulita is quaint yet vibrant. The atmosphere is welcoming and exciting. Accommodations are available everywhere with hotels and Airbnbs ranging from $60 to $150 a night, depending on the time of year. As you walk through the town you get an authentic taste of Mexico. (Of course, there has been a boom in the tourist economy in recent years mainly due to surfing.) While we walked through the market street, we were haggled to buy a sombrero or some other trinkets, and of course we did. The underlying feeling of the place was of an authentic Mexican fishing village, but the truth was we were in a sea of American tourists. The boom also brought expatriates to live in Sayulita. As I was told by an old local fisherman, there is an area of town where Americans live that goes by the name "Gringo Hill."

The first time we stepped on the beach at Sayulita we were greeted by peeling, chest-high rights groomed by a warm offshore wind and green waters. I was later told by another local that the water is actually quite filthy in Sayulita, but I can't say I noticed. It was clear, pleasant, and warm, and I didn't get sick—from the water, at least.
We rented some boards from one of the many shacks along the beach that offer lessons and rentals. The locals were extremely friendly.

The south end of Sayulita is a beach that's great for beginners and surfers seeking smaller waves. In the center and to the north is a reef where waves get progressively larger. We paddled out to the reef and took our place in a lineup that was mainly full of about 10 to 15 visiting surfers. It was late morning, and the waves were great. The reef had some shallow parts, but there was an easy takeoff with a wave that wasn't too fast. The best thing about the first session was the thin crowd, but that changed as they day went on.

As a goofy-footed surfer, going right isn't my favorite thing to do, but I had no choice here. The wave was gentle and sloping at chest height. Being a reef break, it broke pretty consistently through each wave, which was great for gaining confidence and practicing on my backhand. It was beneficial getting some extended standup time with longer rides than I was used to at home in Orange County.

Sayulita is the kind of beach you can spend an entire day at. We paid locals some cash and had a setup on the beach under an awning with a perfect view of the surf. The wind stayed light all day, and the sun was hot. As we sipped beer and ate ceviche in between sessions, it truly felt like any surfer's paradise.

The afternoon session was just as fun but way more crowded. The lineup consisted of locals young and old, male and female. The surf picked up to head-high, and the wave had a little more punch with a slightly steeper takeoff. It was still more than manageable for my average skills with decently lengthed rides and a patient crowd. The younger locals were very good surfers, many riding shortboards and making the most of every inch of a wave. The vibe was still friendly and relaxed. We spoke with many local surfers who were very proud of their breaks and local professional riders. With the luxury of more time, we would have taken up the offer from the locals of a boat trip to some of the better breaks in the area.

The next day the swell was rising, and the waves were a little closed out. There were still some fun waves to be had, but the crowds were unpredictable. Some mornings it was extremely busy, others were more mellow.

Overall, Sayulita is an incredible place for the average surfer. There's a little bit of something for everyone and it has a relaxed and friendly crowd. I would certainly place this locale near the top of your list if you like great seafood, Mexican beer, sunshine, and surfing great waves in boardshorts or a bikini. This place really feels like a tropical surf trip on a budget.

ORANGE COUNTY, CA

Orange County, California—love it or hate it, but you can't deny it that it's the hub of the modern surf industry. All the biggest surf businesses and brands are headquartered in the county, and the surfing population is huge.

I first arrived in California on an unseasonably warm January night in 2007. I was twenty-one and accompanied by my best friend, Phil. We planned for a month of surfing and traveling up and down the Pacific coast. It was the furthest we had ever been from home at the time. California was so iconic to us. As young, impressionable men who lived for surf, weed, music, and fun, we were somewhat starstruck by California. Having grown up in a village of Southern England that lacked youth culture, most of our cultural influences came from California. The music we listened to, the brands we wore, and the boards we rode were all from California. We were in awe of the whole Sublime, surf, beach vibe. Could there have been a better destination for two young men like us at the time? Probably not.

I can still remember the first time I saw California in real life. It was about 10 p.m., and our plane was descending into San Diego airport for its landing. All I could see from my window seat were endless strings of red and yellow lights dancing in the darkness. The freeways looked like sprawling alien spacecrafts. I had never seen so many cars in one place. I remember looking at Phil and laughing out loud with excitement. We had no idea what we were in for, and we were nervous but eager to land.

We stayed in San Diego the first five nights of our trip at The Beach Cottages in Pacific Beach. Pacific Beach was perfect. It was a party town of college students who filled the local bars and clubs. To be fair, Phil and I were not really into the club scene but rather preferred drinking beer at beach bars while the sun set. Although, we did partake in some club activities a few times, including one night when we claimed to be the guitarists from the British band Coldplay. We were promptly given wristbands by club staff and led to the VIP lounge. We didn't even like Coldplay, but it was the only British band we had heard on American radio stations since we had arrived. So, we ramped up the British accents and gladly accepted our invitation to the VIP treatment.

The quickest lesson I learned about Southern California on that trip is that the waves are not world class, not by a long shot. The waves are pretty standard, but that doesn't matter because consistency is king, and when it comes to surf, California is consistent—consistently waist-high and sunny. There are waves most days—they are not always big or clean, but they are there. When it does get good, certain spots can be world class, and there are waves everywhere.

The second lesson I learned about California is regarding the crowded lineups. Before our trip, we read and were told that we wouldn't get waves because it is too crowded, and the vibe was supposed to be very hostile. I have lived in California for ten years now, and I don't find this to be true at all, even for someone like me who is not outwardly competitive or aggressive in the water. I get enough waves, and I have never really had issues regarding localism. I have witnessed hissy fits and shouting matches by overzealous, immature morons but never true localism. I think most people are aware that they are surfing three-foot California, not head-high Pipeline.

California seems to be the epicenter of the average surfer. There are many surfers who you could describe as posers if you were so inclined. When the waves get bigger those surfers are nowhere to be seen, and the lineups thin out. In the summer you can expect a circus, much like anywhere else in the world these days. Somehow though, there still seems to be an order in the water, and there are waves to be had for everyone. Even in Huntington Beach, with clean, three-foot waves, I can find peaks to myself down the beach. With seven miles of sand, I don't need to sit on top of everyone else.

There are plenty of choices when it comes to waves in California. The U.S., in general, is full of choices— too many choices, really. It's the land of choice and consumption. I still laugh when my very British mother comes to visit me, and we go out to eat. It's amusing to see the panic on her face when the waitress asks what type of toast she would like or what kind of milk she would like in her tea. Where my mom comes from, toast is white or brown and milk is from a cow. In California, the waitress will recite an arm-length's list of breads: *bagel, English muffin, wheat, white, sourdough, rye, pumpernickel, farmhouse, whole grain, 9 grain, blah, blah, blah*. It's the same story for most things in America—you can get what you want, when you want, with a smile. It's a little overwhelming at times for a village lad like myself.

I don't mind having choices when it comes to waves, though. While there is not a huge difference in setups, like reefs or point breaks, there are numerous beach breaks up and down Southern California, especially in San Diego and Orange County, some of which are incredibly fun in the right conditions.

My first introduction to surfing in Orange County was, ironically, in Huntington Beach—the place I would find myself living just five or so years later. I remember sitting down on the giant stairs situated on the north side of the pier, watching the madness. As a starstruck kid from Southern England I found it to be so bright and fun. I saw preachers, drum circles, beggars, and buskers; it was complete madness. The surf looked crappy, and we were hungover, so we gave it a pass that day. Instead, we opted to eat sushi for the first time. I loved it, and it quickly became my favorite food. Phil, on the other hand, did not feel the same way as I did. He ordered a tuna roll, and being the Englishman that he is, he thought he was getting a tuna sandwich. His face displayed a perfect mixture of shock and embarrassment when his order of sushi arrived at our table. He didn't' want to be rude, so he hid the tuna roll in his bag and threw it in the trash on our way out. He still hates sushi today.

Unlike ordering food, surfing is easy in Orange County. That's probably why there are so many surfers. You don't need to have any real knowledge of weather patterns, you don't need to have much local knowledge, and there is little searching or adventure involved. You simply check the forecast app on your phone, get in your car, drive to your desired beach, pay the meter, and paddle out. Obviously, for a more advanced surfer, knowledge of tides, winds, and swell direction always helps. If you're looking for adventure, Orange County is not the place. If you're looking for consistent surf, great times with friends, warmish water, and the potential for great waves, Orange County is great.

Orange County is more about icons than anything, including iconic surf spots. Let's start with the most famous of them all—Trestles. Trestles is a stretch of beach that borders Orange County and San Diego in San Clemente. For me, this is the only break in Orange County that still holds some sort of romance and adventure. The adventure being the walk down to the beach; it's a good twenty-minute stroll through a state park and over train tracks. Once you get to the beach, you're greeted by one of the only beaches in the area that is not bordered by city streets and buildings. It is quite pleasant to surf with some of the natural environment on display, even though you can still see the freeway and a nuclear power plant from the lineup. After all, you are still in Southern California.

As for the wave itself, it is as crowded as you've heard. There are numerous waves on that stretch of beach, Lowers being the most famous and busy. On the busiest days it is almost not worth paddling out unless you are willing to paddle battle numerous professionals and young competitive upstart groms. The standard of surfing is also very high.

If I am surfing Trestles, Upper Trestles is my go-to most days. The wave is really fun but with half the crowd. The takeoff is relatively easy, and the wave peels off down the line with a fun ramp that is ideal for all types of surfing. The cobblestone and sand bottom make it easily one of the most fun waves to surf in Southern California.

From Trestles you can take a short drive down the 5 freeway to surf at the legendary San Onofre State Beach, another iconic surf spot. This is really a logging wave, although when it is a little bigger I have had some fun sessions on twin fin fishes and funboards here. Crowds are a bit of an issue here, although they seem to regulate themselves with beginners sticking to the inside and standup paddle boarders having their own designated zone on the south end. San Onofre can be a really fun day out with friends and family as you can pull your car right up to the sand and BBQ all day. The worst thing about San Onofre is the rock dance you'll be forced to perform at low tide when you walk out and in from the waves. For some stubborn reason I refuse to wear booties in California, and I pay the price every time at San Onofre.

Other spots worth visiting for surf in Southern California are Newport, Huntington, and San Clemente. These are all beach breaks where the crowds can be heavy, but you can find your own peak most days, or at the very least you'll only share with a few other surfers. As always, remember to respect the unwritten rules of the lineup, respect the locals, and respect the towns. The beach communities in California are some of the only towns left with some identity and character.

COSTA RICA

There is a variable plethora of travelers and explorers roaming Earth these days. I meet all types of people while on surf trips around the globe—the soul searchers, the retired couples, the holiday makers, and, of course, the surfers. The list is endless. Traveling is more appealing, trendy, and accessible than ever before, and there is nothing wrong with that at all. We can fit all these different types of travelers and explorers into two groups: those who can afford it and those who can't but do it anyway. I fall into the second category. I spend most of my spare cash on travel and sacrifice other things people might call luxuries. I also don't have kids, so that helps. Recently, on average, I manage to take three international trips a year, which is obtainable to anyone who prioritizes correctly.

The latest adventure was planned as a trip for Steph's birthday. Three months prior, I began researching the best place for us to go on an all-out adventure, somewhere neither of us had been. She loves hiking, yoga, working out, and surfing, so based off those activities, I thought where better than Costa Rica. After doing a little more research I concluded, where better than *Nosara*, Costa Rica.

So, there we sat, a few months later, on an Alaskan Airlines flight from Los Angeles to the Liberia Airport. We were flying blind, not knowing much about Nosara other than hearing it offered great hiking and good waves and was a mecca for yogis. I had also heard it was a little less touristy than the more famous surfing destinations in Costa Rica, mainly due to the fact that there isn't a paved road for twenty miles surrounding main beach towns.

We arrived on a Saturday afternoon on the last weekend of May, the start of the down season for tourism; in other words, the wet season. We slipped through customs easily with one backpack each and a board bag. We walked out of the terminal and inhaled our first breath of warm, humid air. It was raining. Hard.

A long line of travel reps and taxi drivers were trying to woo us outside the airport terminal. As they spotted the board bag they'd yelled things like "surfs up, brah," and threw us shakas while promising to take us to the best waves. We eventually settled with Rolando, a mild-mannered tico who was happy to drive us a bumpy two-and-a-half hours to our Airbnb in Playa Guiones. We arrived late in the evening in pouring, warm rain and eventually found the surf shack we had booked. We arranged for Rolando to pick us up in six days, said goodbye, and settled in.

I was pleasantly surprised with Playa Guiones. It's quite hard to define as a place. While it had its fair share of visitors, at first glance it seemed the only people visiting were core surfers and yogis. There were no real holidaymaker tourists. I would imagine the journey into the beach areas would discourage a lot of people. Nosara was a pothole-riddled drive that required a 4x4 or nothing.

The next morning, we rented a quad bike and began to explore. We paddled out at Playa Guiones with chest-high waves and a dark cloud cover. The water felt like a warm bath, and the crowd was thin, probably due to the relentless onshore mess that was presenting itself that morning. It began to rain some of the heaviest rain I have ever seen in my life, even having grown up in England. Being amongst the elements and surfing in a tropical downpour was a fulfilling experience, even though the waves were awful.

Over the next few days, we discovered more waves offered in the area. The rest of the trip was a sunny 85 degrees with the occasional tropical shower. The waves were chest-high and clean most mornings. I have to say the waves in the area are great, there is something for everyone. Playa Guiones must be the most suitable wave for an average surfer that I have ever surfed. What it lacks in punch it makes up for in consistency. I was riding a 5'10 Fitzroy Panda, a wide nosed cheater shortboard with plenty of speed on fat waves. It was perfect for Playa Guiones. Based on surf and waves, I would highly recommend Nosara for the average surfer.

Steph and I are part-time adventure seekers; we work our butts off but always make time to be outside and live. It was our time to go all-out during the six days we spent in Nosara, and we did exactly that. Having the quad was a great idea, we took it everywhere and abused it as much as one should when renting a quad bike in a foreign land. On day three, we went on an off-road quad adventure tour with a local guide named John, a weather-beaten expat from the U.S. who liked surfing and beer. The tour was four hours long with stops in the valleys and mountains, river crossings, and at a local village to stop at what I assumed to be John's mistress's house for a few cans of beer. It didn't seem like a professional tour but more of a "my mate John will take ya, he knows all the best places" kind of tour, and it was all the better for it.

The next few days were spent surfing, exploring, practicing yoga, and even taking some Muay Thai training. I broke my foot at the latter the day before we were due to fly home. Because of that, I can also highly recommend the local Costa Rican pharmacies for painkillers and crutches.

I absolutely love Nosara. I would say that it is the best place I have visited so far on my average surfer travels. But—yes, there is a but—something bugs me deep down. I can't quite put my finger on it. I think it is anxiety and fear of what's to come in Nosara.

The stereotypes in Nosara are almost comical. You don't have to search far to meet all the characters you would expect in such a town. A native Hawaiian I once met on the Big Island described these stereotypes best to me as "trust fund hippies." These are people who live "off the grid" because they are tired of society, yet they are heavily bankrolled by…who knows?

I think my fear for the future of Nosara came from my conversations with the locals. You can feel the dilemma they face. Development seems good at first when you see the boutique surf camps and yoga studios, the juice bars, and the resorts that bring plenty of jobs, but where is the line? I would say Nosara is at the line. Stop now or lose what makes it great. What makes Nosara great is a delicate balance of everything it has—yogis, surfers, bars, wildlife, unpaved roads, and most of all, locals. The local Tico culture is what sets the tone in Nosara. Every step towards future development, however well-intentioned, is a step away from what the town really is and a step towards a Waikiki-like resort town.

Paving the roads in Nosara will bring more casual tourists, and casual tourists demand comfort and convenience, which in turn will bring the next high rise, resort, and so on and so forth.

Right now, Nosara is the perfect balance of off-the-grid adventure and traveler comfort. You can still be on a dirt road adventure amongst snakes and crocodiles, feeling like you're a million miles from civilization. Then, a few short hours later, you can park your quad in a mud puddle of a dirt track and grab a craft beer and the best ahi tuna you've ever had. I say leave it as is and only attract visitors who *really* want to be there. It's a truly special place right now.

FINAL THOUGHTS

In the end, this book became a source of therapy for me because, for me, writing is like any other creative pastime. Some might paint pictures, take photographs, play music, or dance; whatever the creative outlet, I feel there is a need to expel our creativity from our minds and bodies—expel in a good way. We can't let our creativity stew inside us for too long, or we get frustrated and stressed. Creativity acts as purpose, so when I put pen to paper or start cracking away at a keyboard, it becomes a creative outlet for the many thoughts rushing around my mind. Once the thoughts are almost tangible on the computer screen, I feel better, lighter, and happier. I'm no Shakespeare, but that doesn't matter.

I had never written anything of meaning before I

published the "Surfing, Depression and Identity" article on *The Inertia* in 2015. Other than what I learned in high school, I am not formally educated in English or writing. For some reason, back then, I felt compelled to write about my thoughts and feelings. The timing coincided with my depression starting to lift and my new journey beginning. We all go through chapters in our lives, just like a book. For me, that chapter was both the worst and best of my life.

The chapter began on a mild, dark, moonless night in April of 2014. My life had fallen apart roughly a year or so earlier. On that night, at about 3 a.m., I found myself sitting on a river jetty near Newport Beach with a loaded Glock 17 hand gun in my backpack. I had reached the coastline after walking over ten miles in a state of absolute hopelessness. There I sat, at the end of the Earth, on a cold rock, staring at the waves. The black, oil-paint-like ocean would be the only witness. I began to wonder what the news reports might say about the unknown man who was found washed up on the beach at the start of summer.

I sat for hours and thought about my friends, my family, my past, and my future. I thought about the people who had wronged me and the people I had wronged. In the end, I never found enough courage to be a coward that night. I never pulled the trigger and wrote that final chapter.

Instead, my chapter continued. For a while it continued in the same dark setting as I struggled to find a way forward and wondered what I really had to offer myself and the world. I never thought that chapter would end, but it did.

The end of that chapter came on a humid, rainy day in Costa Rica in 2018. I remember a feeling of absolute bliss, absolute contentment, and absolute presence in a moment. Four years after I had been sitting on the rock jetty, there I was, sitting on the back of a quad bike, racing through a jungle to check the surf with my best friend, Steph, at the wheel. I was the happiest I had ever been in my life. How had the story changed so drastically?

The answer was that I had embraced the change. I had gone through everything necessary to learn and to change, including the pain, the hard times, and that night in Newport Beach—not by choice, it was a natural, organic progression. I hadn't forced myself back into a life that led me to depression. I let life show me where to go, led by one of the greatest gifts I had—my love for surfing.

This book was my own creative outlet as I walked through that chapter of my life. I first let go of the depression and then decided to give as much to surfing as it would give to me. I decided to no longer be content with my intermediate skill level.

My surfing and my life became parallels and metaphors of each other. I worked hard on myself, and I worked hard on my surfing. I surfed, I wrote, I loved, I worked, I grafted, I traveled, and, most importantly, I created balance. Today, I find myself the happiest I have ever been.

ABOUT THE AUTHOR

Simon Short is the author of the viral article "A Story about Surfing, Depression and Identity." Simon grew up in England and now lives in Huntington Beach, California. He is a former law enforcement officer turned writer and surf school owner. Simon contributes articles for numerous sports magazines and websites, including *The Inertia*. Most days you can find him surfing somewhere north of Huntington Beach pier.

You can view The Adventures of an Average Surfer at www.surfers.guide

Custom handmade surfboards by www.fitzroysurfboards.com

Follow on Instagram @average_surfers_guide

NOTES

Source Notes

https://www.psychologytoday.com/us/basics/addiction

JeffFoster-https://www.livewithoutacenter.com

https://ideas.ted.com/science_of_freediving/

NOW GO SURF!

59497313R00080

Made in the USA
Columbia, SC
04 June 2019